Their influence on his life
as an Anglican

John Henry Newman: the Liturgy and the Breviary

Their influence on his life
as an Anglican

Donald A. Withey

Sheed & Ward
London

 First published 1992, this edition 1996. ISBN 0 7220 4611 1. Printed and bound in Great Britain for Sheed & Ward Ltd, 14 Coopers Row, London EC3N 2BH by Biddles Ltd, Guildford and King's Lynn.

In memory of
Bernard Basset, SJ
d. 13 June 1988

Contents

List of Illustrations

Acknowledgements

I am grateful to Father Gregory Winterton, Superior of the Birmingham Oratory, for his encouragement and for permission to print hitherto unpublished letters and hymn translations. I am particularly indebted to Gerard Tracey, Archivist and Librarian of the Birmingham Oratory, for much advice and assistance given generously, patiently and unstintingly. Needless to say, he is not to be held responsible for the shortcomings of this book.

I thank the Warden and Fellows of Keble College for allowing me to examine the Keble family letters, and the Librarian, Mrs Jean Robinson, for her kind assistance; the President and Fellows of Magdalen College for allowing me to examine the Bloxam folios, and the Archivist, Mrs Brenda Parry-Jones, for her kind assistance; Miss Lorna Williamson, Librarian of Newman College, Birmingham, for the use of the College's Newman Collection and for arranging some invaluable inter-library loans; Mr Brian Wicks, Director of the Resources Department, Newman College, Birmingham, for his assistance with photography; and last, but certainly not least, my wife for her patience and encouragement during the protracted writing of this book and for her help in checking manuscripts and proofs.

I dedicate my book to the memory of Father Bernard Basset, SJ, whose interest in Newman and Littlemore was well known. I am indebted to him for my initial interest in this subject and for helping me when I began my search for source material.

Cheltenham

Preface

As an Anglican, John Henry Newman is chiefly remembered for his concern with the condition of the Church of England in his own day and for his efforts to regain for that Church a realisation of her catholicity. The effects of the Oxford Movement and the reasons for his eventual disillusionment with the Church of England have often been discussed in the vast literature on Newman.

There are, however, two areas which have been largely neglected: the sense of liturgy which Newman developed as an Anglican, and his encounter with the Roman Breviary. In this book, both of these topics are given detailed examination and appraisal. Some of the ground of the first of these has been covered by Alf Härdelin and Placid Murray, but the topic is given a more extended treatment here. Newman's encounter with the Roman Breviary receives a passing mention in a few works, but its significance has never been fully explored. No comprehensive account of the tortuous history of the Breviary translation project has previously been written. In the very few references to this project in books about Newman, the treatment is scanty and mostly inaccurate. In the final chapter, there is an assessment of the significance of these two topics with regard to Newman's leaving the Church of England and joining the Church of Rome in 1845.

Much of this book is based on a considerable body of unpublished letters and manuscripts of Newman's notes on the Breviary, office hymn translations, and sermons. An extensive range of material was made available to me in the archives of the Birmingham Oratory, and I am particularly grateful for the opportunity of using the complete register of Newman's

Anglican sermons and a copy of the single fascicule of the Breviary translation which was all that was ever printed. (I have been able to trace only two copies of the latter, and I would be grateful for the assistance of readers in tracing other extant copies.) The Keble family letters held at Keble College and the Bloxam folios held at Magdalen College, Oxford, have also been examined.

The text of the ten translations by Newman of Latin office hymns are published for the first time: they are transcribed from Newman's manuscript notebooks in the archives of the Birmingham Oratory.

PART ONE

Newman, the Liturgy and the Roman Breviary

CHAPTER ONE

Beginnings

In November 1821 John Henry Newman conceived the 'audacious idea', as he termed it, of standing for a fellowship at Oriel College, Oxford.[1] Oriel at that time had a leading reputation among the Oxford colleges and followed an enlightened policy in offering its prestigious fellowships to open competition. Newman's success in this demanding examination not only redeemed his poor attainment in the Schools but brought him into the circle of outstanding men in the Senior Common Room at Oriel. His election to the fellowship in April 1822 was a turning point in his career and in his religious development. He had come up to Oxford in 1816 an earnest young Christian imbued with evangelical and Calvinistic principles. His upbringing as a 'middle of the road' Anglican with a great devotion to the Bible was followed during his years at school firstly by a period of adolescent doubt and then, under the influence of Walter Mayers, a master at the school, by a type of conversion experience and the acceptance of the doctrines of election and imputed righteousness.

At Oriel he encountered liberal theology and the intellectual rigour and questioning of the 'Noetics'. The influence on him of men such as Whately and Hawkins was very significant. Whately brought him out of his shyness and awkwardness, encouraged him to think independently and taught him to regard the Church as a visible body and to reject Erastianism. Richard Whately's views on logic were also an influence on Newman. Edward Hawkins taught him the significance of tradition in Christian belief and was also in time to draw Newman away finally from Calvinism.

During the summer of 1824 both Hawkins and Newman

stayed up at Oxford because of their parochial duties, Hawkins being vicar of St Mary's and Newman curate of St Clement's. Newman showed Hawkins his sermons, receiving in return rigorous criticism of them, especially of his dividing line between the 'saved' and the 'unsaved'. It is significant how much Newman learnt from practical pastoral experience. Up to about 1822 he had found it impossible to accept the doctrine of baptismal regeneration because of the sinful lives and lack of holiness of so many people after their baptism. This conviction arose largely from his observation of other people, and in his own case he felt certain that baptism had not affected him in the way his 'conversion' of 1816 had. At St Clement's, however, he learnt from more precise experience, especially as he carried out his systematic visitation of his parishioners. He came to see that the doctrine of election simply did not make sense: people could not be neatly divided into the categories of 'saved' and 'unsaved'.

The influence of Hawkins was reinforced by pastoral experience, and by 1827 Newman had abandoned belief in election and had accepted baptismal regeneration. About this time also he was introduced to the doctrine of apostolic succession by another Fellow of Oriel, William James.

Newman's mind was now prepared for his encounter with Richard Hurrell Froude and John Keble. Froude became a Fellow of Oriel in 1826. Keble was nine years older than Newman and had been a Fellow of Oriel since 1811. A close friendship developed between Newman and the two men, and Newman began to adopt some of Froude's High Church views because they accorded closely with his own growing conception of the Church.

Froude was proud of having brought Newman and Keble together. Newman had stood in some awe of Keble for his academic brilliance, his asceticism and reserve, and above all for his holiness and prayerful life. Now he came to value the friendship and influence of the older man. From this time Keble was closely involved in Newman's development. The influence of Keble's traditional High Church views was due not only to the growing friendship between the two men but also to *The Christian Year* which Keble published in 1827. Newman paid tribute to this work in his *Apologia*.[2] In particular he learnt from it to revere the sacramental system, the communion of saints, and the mysteries of the faith.

Between 1825 and 1827 Newman moved away from Evangelicalism. At this time his reading of Butler's *Analogy* reinforced his growing acceptance of the sacramental principle and the concept of the visible Church. From Butler also he came to see the historical character of revelation. At the same time he passed through a period of disdain for antiquity and an inclination towards rationalism. He was abruptly rescued from this frame of mind by illness (an attack of nervous exhaustion) in November 1827 and by the sudden death of his sister Mary in January 1828. This phase in his development was brought to completion by his systematic reading of the Fathers of the Church which he commenced in July 1828. As part of this he made a particular study of Arianism, and became profoundly engaged in considering the nature of the Church. The most significant factor in Newman's theological development was his progressive acceptance of the Church as a divinely founded institution, acting and teaching with authority, and based on the sacraments. He now had the foundation for the developed ecclesiology which enabled him to view the Church of England as part of the 'Church Catholic', holding an intermediate position between modern Romanism and modern Protestantism.

He was also in a position to respond to the apparent danger threatening the Church of England. This danger was two-fold. To Newman, Roman Catholic emancipation had constituted an affront to the Church of England. Now the Whigs were planning to abolish ten Irish bishoprics, and there were threats of disestablishment and of changes by force of legislation to the authority and worship of the Church. This utter disregard for the divinely founded Church, evidenced by the intention of the government to legislate for it as if it were a mere department of state, was to be found among many of its bishops and priests.

From within the Church, there was, in Newman's judgment, a widespread failure to recognise and live up to the catholicity of the Church of England, especially in regard to the sacraments, the episcopacy, and the apostolic succession. Keble's Assize Sermon on 'The National Apostasy', preached on 14 July 1833, acted on Newman like a call to action. Keble made an appeal for the defence of the Church, especially in view of the proposed abolition of ten Irish bishoprics. This was followed later the same month by a meeting at Hadleigh at which Hugh Rose, Froude, William Palmer and Arthur Perceval discussed these dangers. Newman and Keble were unable to be present, but Froude reported the discussions to them. Newman considered their proposals for an association and for petitions to be inadequate, and in September he took the initiative himself and began the *Tracts for the Times*.

Newman wrote the first three tracts himself. The first and second were very brief and characterised by a note of urgency, entreating the clergy to realise the nature of their ministry and the apostolic and Catholic nature of the Church. In the third Tract Newman argued against alterations to the Prayer Book liturgy: alterations, however well meant, would serve to weaken the Church still further.

The themes of these first three Tracts highlight the main concerns of the Tractarians, which were to be further developed in the remaining eighty-seven Tracts. The Tracts soon grew in size. They ceased to be manifestos and became treatises, especially with Pusey's contributions. Widely circulated, they attracted much attention and exerted considerable influence especially in promoting a sense of the catholicity of the Church of England. Their authors did not want to introduce innovations, but rather to regain for the Church a fuller conception of itself and its worship. A few of the Tracts were on specifically liturgical topics, many more were concerned with the Church and its services, and with the sacraments.[3] A considerable number of Tracts consisted of extracts or reprints of the works of the Fathers and the Anglican divines, and they were designed to show the place of the Church in Catholic tradition.

The Tractarians increasingly identified themselves with the teaching of the Caroline divines and the non-Jurors, finding particularly congenial their view that the Church was essentially Catholic not Protestant, the separation from Rome having occurred for practical purposes. It is significant that the Oxford Movement was responsible, directly or indirectly, for the republication of many of the works of the Anglican divines, most of which had some bearing on liturgical matters. The divines had been well read in the Fathers of the Church and had insisted that the Bible should be interpreted according to patristic teaching. To make the writings of the Fathers available to Anglicans, *The Library of the Fathers of the Holy Catholic Church Anterior to the Division of the East and West* was instituted. Altogether forty-eight volumes were issued during the years 1838 to 1885. They were variously edited by Pusey, Newman, Keble and Marriott, and provided translations of the works of thirteen Fathers.[4]

The concern of the Tractarians with worship was an integral element in their conception of the Church. Their exalted view of episcopacy and priesthood, their insistence on the sacramental principle, their rich eucharistic theology, based on the Incarnation and inspired by patristic teaching, and their desire to reinstate the full observation of the Prayer Book services made liturgy inseparable from the institutional aspects of the 'Church Catholic'. It was especially in the liturgy of the communion service and the daily offices that they discerned, thanks to a revival of liturgical studies, a strong sign of that continuity with the pre-Reformation Church which they were professing.

CHAPTER TWO

Newman and the Liturgy

Despite the ritualism associated with the later history of the Oxford Movement, the Tractarians were not interested in ceremonial or ritualistic innovations. Their concern was to restore a full observation of the existing liturgy of the Prayer Book. Ironically, they were regarded as dangerous innovators for advocating the frequent celebration of Holy Communion and the daily celebration of the offices. They were associated with the revival of interest in liturgical studies which took place in the first half of the nineteenth century and helped to promote it, although they were not the originators of it.

The revival was foreshadowed by the Bampton Lectures delivered in 1804 by Richard Laurence. He set out to show that the Reformation in England was Lutheran not Calvinist, and in the course of the lectures he provided some useful material on the 1552 Prayer Book and, more particularly, on the baptismal services.[1] It was Charles Lloyd who inaugurated the revival. He became Regius Professor of Divinity in 1822 and his ambition was to preside over a great school of theology at Oxford. He therefore supplemented his public lectures with a series of private lectures to which Newman, Pusey and a limited number of Oxford dons were invited. Lloyd lectured on biblical and doctrinal topics, and had a considerable influence on Newman, Pusey and their associates, his teaching in many ways resembling the main tenets of the Oxford Movement. It was probably not until a later series of lectures that he began to include the topic for which he is chiefly remembered, the content and origins of the Prayer Book services. Lloyd caused much surprise by emphasising the primitive and medieval elements to be found in the Prayer Book, and he introduced his audience to medieval service books.

Froude began attending these lectures in 1827 and he recorded Lloyd's treatment of the liturgy.[2] It seems clear that Froude was greatly inspired by these lectures and that he shared with Newman his enthusiasm for Roman missals and breviaries and for the history of the liturgy. Frederick Oakeley also attended these classes on liturgy and was impressed by the Catholic interpretation which Lloyd gave to the structure of the Book of Common Prayer.[3] The influence of Lloyd's lectures went far beyond the small number of selected graduates who attended them. Newman himself probably did not attend Lloyd's lectures on liturgy, but learnt a great deal about liturgical origins and about the liturgical books still in use in the Latin rite from Froude.[4]

Lloyd had made annotations in the margin of a folio Prayer Book of material for a study of the origins of the English ritual. These were used after Lloyd's early death by William Palmer (of Worcester College), who had not himself attended Lloyd's lectures. In 1832 he published a history of the English Liturgy, *Origines Liturgicae*. In his enthusiasm for missals, breviaries and other service books, Palmer largely ignored the discontinuity in favour of the continuity between the Prayer Book and the older liturgies. However, it was an ambitious work for its time and had much influence. During the next two decades, 'Oxford became the source of a flood of liturgical reprints' and 'the fruits of all this labour were gathered by the Reverend Francis Proctor in his *History of the Book of Common Prayer* (1854).[5] Hitherto it had been generally assumed that the Prayer Book was mainly the work of the English reformers of the sixteenth century. Palmer's description of the eastern and western liturgies, his historical account of the Roman Breviary, his analysis of the origins of the English ritual, and his illustrated appendix on vestments[6] came as something of a revelation to most of his contemporaries. Bookshops began to stock missals and breviaries to meet a demand for them.

The *Tracts for the Times* played a considerable part in the new interest in liturgy and its origins. The outstanding liturgical Tract was Newman's account of the Roman Breviary (Tract 75) (see Chapter Eight). This Tract was not typical in that it advocated, albeit guardedly, the use by Anglicans of a service book which was distinctively Roman Catholic. Most of the Tracts which had any bearing on liturgy dealt with restoring neglected elements in the Prayer Book. In Tract 9 Froude attacked the idea of shortening the Prayer Book services and pleaded for the reinstatement of daily services. Tom Keble compiled a collection of twenty-seven extracts from the divines and other sources, to support the contention that there should be morning prayer and evening prayer every day in the parish church, which he published as Tract 84. John Keble also opposed change, arguing in Tract 13 for preserving the Sunday lectionary and demonstrating the principles on which it was constructed.

Only Froude can be said to have broken new ground. In Tract 63 he drew on Palmer's *Origines Liturgicae* to show the essential characteristics of the traditional liturgies, with particular reference to the prayers of consecration and oblation. He gave translations of the latter as they are found in the Roman Missal, the Liturgy of St John, the Liturgy of St Mark, and the Gallican liturgy to show that in each of these liturgies 'the Eucharist is regarded as a mystery and a sacrifice'. Froude concluded:

> Such is the view taken of the Consecration and Oblation of the Eucharist in the four independent Christian Liturgies. It is well worth the consideration of such Protestant bodies as have rejected the Ancient Forms.

There was a two-fold thrust in Froude's very restrained criticism here. In the first place he did not wish to classify the Prayer Book as a Protestant compilation but as a member of the family of traditional liturgies. In the second place he was not oblivious, as Palmer seems to have been, to what could be seen as defects in the communion service of the Prayer Book. However he leaves his readers to draw their own conclusions, simply giving a footnote reference to the novel order of the service and an oblique indication of what it lacked, namely a sacrificial oblation, prayers for the dead, the kiss of peace, and the fraction.[7] He was more outspoken in a private letter to Christie in 1834 where he advocated that the communion service be 'replaced by a good translation of the liturgy of St Peter, that is, the *Missale Romanum*'.[8]

When such letters were made public in his *Remains*, Froude's extravagant remarks and his sweeping criticisms caused much offence. Doubtless he discussed his views with Newman, who made allowances for his young friend's exuberance, knowing both his deep spirituality and poor health. In the company of his friends, John Keble was not insensitive to the defects in the Prayer Book which Froude attacked, but he always avoided open criticism of the Church and its institutions, preferring to observe reverence and respect for holy things.

Newman likewise preferred respect to criticism. It took him a long time to reach a position of radical disagreement with some of the characteristics of Anglican liturgy. It was not until 1838 that he was able to propose in his letter to Faussett that the Holy Communion service should be recast in accordance with the Latin Mass and with the restoration of the prayers which had been removed by the reformers.[9] Pusey discussed in Tract 81 the possibility of supplementing the Holy Communion service with prayers from the Missal said silently (an arrangement which later became common Anglo-Catholic practice). But for the most part the reservations held by some of the Tractarians remained private. Their desire to restore and reinstate the Prayer Book services was prior to any desire to reform them. And it is noteworthy that some Tractarians, such as Tom Keble and his associates in the so-called 'Bisley School', found no difficulty in accepting both the Prayer Book without reservation and the work of the sixteenth-century reformers in England and at the same time accommodating both within their High Church views of the Church of England as the 'Church Catholic'.[10] This wing of the Tractarians felt no pull towards Rome and were to be strongly critical of Newman for supporting the Breviary translation project.

For the Tractarians as for Newman, liturgy was integrally related to the Church. In Tract 11, *The Visible Church*, Newman asserted that the unity and corporateness of the

Church is made manifest in the liturgy. The liturgy, he argued, was not an arbitrary arrangement of elements of worship, but an ordering of worship based on the Eucharist and the sacraments. It is significant that one of the apologetic claims made by Pusey in his letter to the Bishop of Oxford in 1839 was that the Tractarians had successfully prevented misconceived reform of the Prayer Book, thereby preserving it and restoring its full use.[11]

For most of his Anglican life, Newman supported in public the Tractarian principle of retaining and restoring the Prayer Book liturgy.[12] His practice was also conservative, with no deviations from the Prayer Book. Throughout his Anglican days he always celebrated Holy Communion at the north end, vested in surplice and hood. For preaching he may sometimes have put on a gown, but more commonly he wore surplice and hood. The well-known print of Newman preaching at St Mary's [13] shows him in surplice and hood. Apparently he was similarly vested for his last sermon at Littlemore,[14] for it is recorded that on leaving the pulpit he took off his hood and flung it over the altar rails. Newman took no part in the revival of ritualism and of vestments; the latter were not in fact adopted in the Anglican Church until after Newman's departure.[15]

In the new church at Littlemore, opened in 1836, Newman had a stone altar and reredos, and behind the altar a stone cross. Otherwise Newman himself did not introduce anything into the new church which might have been considered novel. However, he gave Bloxam, his curate at Littlemore from 1837 to 1840, more or less a free hand in arranging the ornaments and the ceremonial. As a result, Bloxam introduced into the church gilded candlesticks (copies of those in the chapel of Magdalen College), two standard candlesticks, a wooden alms dish, a credence table, a litany desk, and on the altar a bible in two volumes bound in crimson. Most of these features were adopted soon afterwards by Frederick Oakeley in the Margaret Chapel in 1839 and later were to become usual in many Anglican churches.[16]

At St Mary's also Newman had altar candles. He used the

mixed chalice, an ancient practice which was retained in the 1549 Prayer Book but not in subsequent editions. Fanciful explanation of this practice, which was adopted also by other Anglicans in the nineteenth century, were not lacking. One of the more plausible was that some Tractarians, weakened by their Lenten fast, found themselves almost overpowered by the smell of the chalice.[17] Newman himself gave the following explanation in 1864:

> When I began early communion in St Mary's in 1837, one or more communicants applied to me to the effect that the wine was strong and on account of its strength was unpleasant to them the first thing in the morning, and on that account I mixed water with it ... It must be recollected that the so called wine used for the Anglican Communion used to be a strange composition ... I think the sacramental wine at St Mary's was complained of, not so much as getting into men's heads, as having an unpleasant taste in the mouth.[18]

Newman's position can be summed up by saying that while he was not a liturgist, he had a very marked sense of liturgy. He seems, however, to have made very little study of it. One exception to this is his reading in preparation for writing Tract 75. Otherwise his knowledge of liturgical matters came mainly through his discussions with Froude. His only contribution *ex professo* to liturgy was Tract 75, and even here he admits that his work was derivative. He does not seem to have acquired any service books, until he received Froude's breviary as a memento, nor did he buy any works by liturgiologists.[19]

At the same time, liturgy was an integral element in the Tractarian platform. The development of Newman's very marked sense of liturgy can be traced especially in his contributions to the Tracts, in his own pastoral practice, in his sermons, and later in his interest in the Roman Breviary. (The liturgical themes to be found in many of the Tracts, including those by Newman, have already been noted in Chapter One. See also Appendix One. Newman's interest in the Roman Breviary is dealt with in Chapters Three and Eight.)

Newman's liturgical awareness can be seen very clearly in his own pastoral practice. Newman is sometimes thought of as having lived in something of an ivory tower, concerned mainly with writing books and letters. It is the case however, that Newman was for the greater part of his adult life a parish priest. There were very few years from 1824, when he was ordained deacon in the Church of England, until his death in 1890 when he was not actively involved in pastoral duties in an Anglican or Catholic parish. As an Anglican, his reflection on the nature of the 'Church Catholic' strengthened his belief that the Church's worship was at the centre of her life and mission. This belief characterised his pastoral practice, as can be seen in the assiduity with which he conducted services at the church of St Clement, at St Mary the Virgin, Oxford, and at St Mary and St Nicholas, Littlemore. An important part of his visitation of parishioners, which he carried out very systematically, was concerned with church attendance and he encouraged his people to involve themselves in liturgical services because he believed the daily office and frequent celebration of communion to be of the essence of the life of the Church.

The devotion with which he led church services has often been remarked on. He attached great importance to what is now known as the liturgy of the word, and his reading of scripture and his homilies made a lasting impression on those who heard him. Before the church at Littlemore was built, he walked frequently to the village to hold meetings for prayer and instruction, realising that few of the inhabitants could be expected to come to St Mary's in the city. In both the Oxford and the Littlemore ends of his parish, the people now experienced an unprecedented level of pastoral care. The leading feature of this was a measure of liturgical development. In an age when Holy Communion was celebrated infrequently, often only quarterly, Newman instituted a weekly celebration at St Mary's. He had been considering this since 1833. He actually began the practice at Easter 1837: the service was held at 7.00 a.m. and there were thirty-six communicants.[20] Equally neglected was the celebration of the daily offices of Matins and Evensong, despite the clear injunction of the Prayer Book. Newman began the daily celebration of Matins in St Mary's on Monday, 30 June 1834. When the church at Littlemore was opened in 1836, Newman or one of his curates walked there daily to celebrate Evensong.[21] Newman started hearing confessions in Lent 1838. This also was something clearly provided for in the Prayer Book. Newman's concern in restoring Prayer Book services was predominantly pastoral. For him, the liturgy was at the centre of the Church's life: any diminution or minimising of the liturgy was a betrayal of the Church's duty towards God and the people. His pastoral concern in fostering the liturgy is spelt out clearly in Tract 75 and in his sermon 'The Daily Service'.

In an age when sermons were often long, unstimulating and perfunctory, Newman's sermons were outstanding for their spirituality, sincerity and effectiveness. They touched men's hearts, they seemed to speak to the needs and condition of each individual. His motto as a cardinal was *cor ad cor loquitur* and this principle sums up the impact of his sermons. Although the services were parochial in status, large congregations of undergraduates were attracted to his Sunday afternoon service at St Mary's for the sermons: this was one of the chief factors in Newman's fame in Oxford.[22]

Newman's sermons show the high view he held of the Eucharist and of the significance of the eucharistic ministry in the Church. He drew on his deep knowledge of the scriptures and of the Fathers to formulate his conception of the eucharistic mystery. Like most of the Caroline divines he held a belief in the real presence. This belief was held by most of the Tractarians, together with a belief in the Eucharist as sacrificial, though there were some differences of emphasis. These beliefs had their tentative beginning in Newman's early sermons and were to reach their fullest development in Wilberforce's theory of sacramental identity and his belief in the offering of Christ himself in the Eucharist. Another highpoint of this development was Tract 81 (1837) in which Pusey claimed that the ancient view of the Eucharist as an impetratory sacrifice was still Anglican doctrine if the testimony of the Anglican divines was accepted.[23]

The sermons also show a profound sense of liturgical time, centred around the Incarnation and the Paschal mystery. The liturgical year was of major importance to Newman and he often dealt with the seasons and the great feasts in his parochial sermons.[24] Newman also preached numerous sermons in connection with saints' days, especially the apostles, whom he saw as the foundation of the Church. Among his published and unpublished sermons, for example, there were in 1830 sermons on Peter, James the Greater, Barnabas, Bartholomew, Matthew, Mark, Luke, John, and Mary Magdalen.

Apart from seasons and feasts, there were many topics of liturgical concern on which Newman preached. A list of thirty-nine of his Anglican sermons on such topics is given in Appendix Two. Twenty-six of these sermons are at present unpublished. Of particular interest is the course of ten sermons, mostly unpublished, on the liturgy, given on Sundays 31 January to 4 April 1830. In the first of these, Newman discussed the meaning of 'liturgy' and emphasised the eucharistic (thanks-giving) nature of all Christian worship. This theme was continued in the second sermon where he dealt with the necessity of precomposed and authorised prayers in the liturgy and with the merits of the Prayer Book. The next three were concerned with the function of liturgy in teaching doctrine: that is, doctrine about God, man's duty, and the means of grace. The remaining five sermons were concerned with the function of liturgy in forming character, with particular reference to faith, hope, reverence, self-denial, and love. In the ninth sermon he linked self-denial to the Lenten liturgy, and it is interesting to note that Newman placed as much emphasis on Lenten observance in his sermons as in his private life. In the decade 1831 to 1841 he preached forty-one sermons on Lent. In June and July 1828 he gave a course of six sermons on Baptism, Confirmation, and the Lord's Supper. In addition he preached sermons at various times on the sacraments, on prayer, preaching and fasting.

Newman's profound sense of liturgy is to be seen not only in the topics on which he preached but also in the style and structure of his sermons. They were authentic liturgical homilies, being related to the liturgy and based on scripture. In his discussion of Newman's sermons, Placid Murray described them as 'basically dogmatic': they incorporated the traditional patristic theology of the Incarnation, Redemption and the Trinity'. In them

> five basic traits are in evidence throughout: the awareness of the Easter cycle as the great sacramental season: of the eschatological Day inaugurated by the Resurrection of Christ; of the new range of Christian feelings aroused by the mysteries of Christ's life as commemorated in the liturgy; of the presence of the risen Christ to his Church, and of the understanding of sacred history as doctrine.[25]

CHAPTER THREE

Newman and the Breviary

Newman did not possess a breviary until 1836 when he inherited Froude's. It is not known where or when Froude purchased this breviary, but it is likely that he bought it in London or Oxford as a result of hearing about the Breviary at Lloyd's lectures which he attended in 1827–8. Isaac Williams, later to be Newman's curate at St Mary's, vouched for the fact that breviaries were acquired by a number of Oxford men as a result of Lloyd's lectures:

> Bishop Lloyd, then the Divinity Professor, was giving lectures on the Prayer-book, and referring men to the sources from whence the Prayer-book was taken, and in particular to the breviaries, on account of which copies of them were procured from a Roman Catholic bookseller in London.[1]

This bookseller was probably Booker in New Bond Street. Frederick Oakeley recalled the effect on Booker's trade of Lloyd's lectures on the Prayer Book:

> On a sudden, and without explained cause, Mr Booker's repository, in New Bond street, was taxed even to the full extent of its ample resources, to furnish liturgies, and office books, for the Oxford students. Mr Booker was too good a Catholic to treat such a demand as a mere matter of business, and, as he dared not hope for a miracle, shrewdly suspected a plot. By a singular coincidence it happened that the only Protestant in Oxford whom Mr Booker knew was myself, and that the only Catholic in the world whom I knew was Mr Booker; and I believe I was the means of allaying his apprehensions, and securing a free importation of Missals and Breviaries into Oxford.[2]

William Parker was also known to be selling Roman and Parisian breviaries in Oxford in 1840.[3]

It soon became a common practice to purchase breviaries on holiday on the Continent. George Prevost acquired a four volume Parisian Breviary in Paris, which was passed on to Isaac Williams in 1829, who in turn showed it to John Keble.[4] Others associated with Newman bought breviaries in France, Belgium or Italy. Some of the breviaries used at Littlemore were acquired in this way. One volume of Dalgairns's breviary, published in Paris, is preserved today at Littlemore.

Frederick William Faber related in a letter to J. B. Morris how he and R. W. Church toured Europe in 1839 and bought themselves breviaries:

> I determined, and so did Church, to conform to the Catholic ritual here. We both of us got Mechlin Breviaries at Mechlin, and go to church pretty regularly every day to say the Hours, and we say the rest of the Hours as the priests do in carriages or inns or anywhere. Also I have been tutorised in the Breviary by a very *nice* priest, a simple hearted, pious fellow, with little knowledge of theology.[5]

William George Ward characteristically took to the Breviary on his own initiative. He had a great admiration for Roman Catholic liturgy and often went to the Catholic Chapel in Spanish Place for Mass instead of attending the Anglican Holy Communion 'long before he joined the Puseyite party'.[6] In his recollections of Ward, Edward Goulburn wrote:

> I remember that the greater variety of the Breviary Services attracted him, and was the subject of his admiration, long before he made up his mind to quit the communion of the English Church ...[7]

Liddon recorded that Pusey began using the Sarum Breviary from about 1839 as a supplement to the offices of the Prayer Book.[8]

Froude owed his interest in the Roman Breviary firstly to Lloyd and then to Blanco White. Newman himself does not seem to have had much contact with White, but many of his friends did, especially in the years 1826 and 1827. Discussions with White were a stimulating experience and his views provided a considerable insight into Roman Catholicism. As an ex-priest he was familiar with the Roman Breviary and enjoyed explaining how to use it to his Oriel friends in his rooms after dinner. He recorded in his journal for 31 October 1827: 'Pusey, Wilberforce, and Froude came in the evening to learn the order of the Roman Catholic Service of the Breviary.'[9] There is no evidence that Newman himself attended these sessions conducted by White, and, as already argued (see Chapter Two), it is improbable that he attended any lectures on the Prayer Book and its origins given by Dr Lloyd.[10] He did not have any interest in the Breviary until after Froude's death, and then, using Froude's breviary, he taught himself how to use it.

Froude, on the other hand, had a greater interest in Catholic practices. With Blanco White's guidance, he evidently studied the Breviary in detail and presumably used it regularly: at least when his health permitted. He went to the West Indies on one of several trips abroad for the sake of his health, staying there from November 1833 until May 1835. In a letter to John Keble from Barbados dated 2 May 1834 he asked for certain books to be sent to him, including 'the parts autumnalis and hyemalis of my Breviary'[11] The breviary reached him in Barbados, according to a reference in Newman's *Apologia*,[12] and in a letter dated 25 February 1835 Froude wrote to Keble:

> I can see no other claim which the Prayer Book has on a Layman's deference, as the teaching of the Church, which the Breviary and Missal have not in a far greater degree.[13]

Froude and Newman must have discussed the Breviary from time to time. During his last illness Froude wrote to Newman from Dartington on 2 December 1835: 'N. B. Harpsfield is the writer on the Breviary services whose name I could not remember.'[14]

Once again Froude left his breviary behind at Oriel and asked in a letter dated 10 December 1835 '. . . if he (Rogers) will bring my breviary I shall be obliged'[15] This letter to Newman accompanied a review for the *British Critic* of a book, ironically by Blanco White: 'Mr Blanco White: Heresy and Orthodoxy'. The man who had taught him how to use the Breviary had joined the Unitarians the previous January. Frederic Rogers (later Lord Blachford), a pupil of Froude and of Newman, had been invited to spend Christmas 1835 at Dartington. He travelled down there on the same day that Froude's article and letter were received by Newman, 14 December.[16] He did not, in the event, take the breviary, which was still on the shelves of Froude's room at Oriel after his death on 28 February 1836. Archdeacon Froude wrote to Newman on that same Sunday evening to tell him of Hurrell Froude's death, adding:

> . . . there are some books and other things left by poor Hurrell in his rooms . . . Will you my dear Mr. N. select any things you please as a token of remembrance from your departed friend?

Newman later annotated this letter as follows: 'N.B. I chose, at the suggestion of Rogers, his Breviary. J.H.N.'[17] Newman's response to this invitation is recorded in the *Apologia*:

> At a comparatively early date I drew up the tract on the Roman Breviary . . . It was an apparent accident which introduced me to the knowledge of that most wonderful and most attractive monument of the devotion of saints. On Hurrell Froude's death, in 1836, I was asked to select one of his books as a keepsake. I selected Butler's *Analogy*: finding that it had been already chosen, I looked with some perplexity along the shelves as they stood before me, when an intimate friend at my elbow said, 'Take that.' It was the Breviary which Hurrell had had with him at Barbados. Accordingly I took it, studied it, wrote my tract from it, and have it on my table in constant use till this day. That dear and familiar companion, who thus put the Breviary into my hands, is still in the Anglican Church.[18]

The breviary, which is preserved at the Birmingham Oratory, is in four volumes, the pages of which measure 5¾ inches x 3¼ inches. It was published at Antwerp by the Plantin Press in 1823. It is a plain and undistinguished edition with small print and few illustrations. It shows signs of much use such as foxing, the gold worn on spine lettering (though not on decoration on front and back covers), and the front board on the first volume (Pars Autumnalis) loose. On the flyleaf of the latter is inscribed in small neat handwriting by Newman:

> John H. Newman
> March 12 1836
> This Breviary, which belonged
> to Richard Hurrell Froude, was
> given to me by William Froude on
> R.H.F.'s death

Newman continued using Froude's breviary after 1845. He acquired various other breviaries during his Catholic days, beginning with a set purchased in Rome in 1846, and including a set inherited from William Henry Scott in 1859.[19] His collection of breviaries is on a table behind the smaller (sloped) writing desk near the window of Newman's room.

Froude also knew and loved the Parisian Breviary and its hymns, although it is not known whether he possessed his own copy. It was fitting that Newman and Keble should have prefixed to Froude's *Remains* a verse from a Parisian Breviary hymn, *Se sub serenis vultibus* ...[20]

Newman always regarded the acquisition of Froude's breviary as one of the landmarks in his development. When arranging his letters, he attached the following note to one of the bundles:

> Memorandum: March 1836
> March 1836 is a cardinal point of time. It gathers about it, more or less closely, the following events:
>
> 1. Froude's death.
> 2. My Mother's death and my Sister's marriage.
> 3. My knowing and using the Breviary.
> 4. First connexion with the *British Critic*.
> 5. The tracts become treatises.
> 6. Start of the Library of the Fathers.
> 7. Theological Society.
> 8. My writing against the Church of Rome.
> 9. Littlemore Chapel.[21]
>
> } A new scene gradually opened

From this time he began to study the Breviary and compiled Tract 75. In a footnote in the *Remains* Newman wrote of the Tract:

> . . . the idea and groundwork . . . was the Author's [Froude's], but the MS containing it in too imperfect a state to publish.[22]

Newman told Albany Christie that this was

> . . . the Tract on the Breviary which I published, not supposing it would answer but because dear Froude wished it.[23]

The manuscript by Froude to which Newman refers has not survived, and Newman made no further reference to it in his notes and draft for the Tract. While Froude may have made the original suggestion for the Tract and compiled some rough notes, it seems clear from Newman's papers that, having studied Froude's breviary, he went to the Bodleian Library on 2 May 1836 and made notes from two works, Bartolomeo Gavanti's *Thesaurus Sacrorum Rituum* (1628) and Francesco Zaccaria's *Bibliotheca Ritualis* (two volumes, 1776 and 1781). These notes, preserved in the Birmingham Oratory archives, were the basis on which Newman composed the Tract.[24]

He also began using the Breviary offices as part of his daily prayer. He omitted such elements as the invocation of the Virgin Mary and the saints and the Marian antiphons as being against the teaching and practice of the Church of England. He stopped making these omissions in his private recitation of the Breviary soon after the publication of Tract 90.[25] His attachment to the Breviary was such that he began to record in his diary from 11 February 1837 the days on which he failed to recite some or all of the Hours.[26] It would seem that he recited the offices slowly. 'The Breviary Devotions take up from 3 to 4 hours a day,' he told Wilberforce.

> I like them uncommonly. They are very unexciting, grave and simple. They are for the whole year, varying day by day more or

> less. This again I like much; it keeps up attention and rouses the imagination towards the course of the Christian year, without exciting it ... Latin devotions are majestic and austere ... they are better fitted for praise and earnest expostulation. The great advantage of a dead language is that it keeps one sober.[27]

The Breviary continued to be significant to Newman. It may be that, as Edwin Abbott put it, Froude's breviary which Newman used daily and kept on his desk symbolised the continuing influence of the friend he had lost.[28]

CHAPTER FOUR

The Breviary Translation Project – Phase One

Tract 75, published in June 1836, proved to be an unexpected success. 'To my astonishment,' Newman wrote to Frederic Rogers on 7 January 1837,

> Rivington has just sent me word that the tract on the Breviary is coming to a second edition . . . Rivington had told me that the tracts were selling well, but 750 copies of the 'Roman Breviary' since July last is portentous.[1]

'How very interesting is the Breviary Tract!' exclaimed Henry Wilberforce,[2] and his view was shared by many Anglicans.

This interest was widespread, and early in 1838 two young friends of Newman, Samuel Wood and Robert Williams, formed a plan to translate the Roman Breviary. The project had been the subject of conversation among the Tractarians living in London (Wood, Williams, Thomas Dyke Acland, John William Bowden, James Robert Hope-Scott, Edward Badeley, and Gladstone were some of the leading Tractarians there) for about a year before Newman became involved. Keble did not become involved until later. The plan was for the translation to be published privately in instalments and to be purchased by subscription.

Newman's friends were both laymen. Samuel Wood, an Oriel man, was a barrister at the Inner Temple and brother of the future first Lord Halifax. Shortly before his early death, Wood helped to buy the stable block at Littlemore. Robert Williams, also an Oriel man, lived in London and was MP for Dorchester from 1835 to 1841. He often caused offence to his friends by his supercilious manner of speaking about things held to be sacred by Anglicans. His Romanist tendencies in these years (he later moved over to the Evangelical wing of the Church) also caused concern.[3]

The project had a tortuous history and was revived twice before it was finally dropped, the main events of the first phase occurring in 1838. It first came to Newman's knowledge when he received a letter from Rogers dated 26 January 1838:

> Has Wood told you that he and R.W. [Williams] talk of publishing a translation of the Breviary (or greater part of it) in monthly(?) numbers by subscription. He wishes to do it in an independent way without committing you or anybody else so perhaps he has not . . .[4]

It seems that Newman wrote to Wood on the subject, presumably supporting the project in principle but foreseeing certain difficulties, for Wood replied to Newman on 5 February:

> Robert Williams has been translating since last summer, and on his showing me a specimen I found it quite well and closely enough done to form a good basis for correction, and undertook to take the Commons and otherwise to help him. Supposing us to finish this summer what we think of is this: Two months before the Church-year begins to bring out, first the Psaltery, next the Commons, and then on the 1st of each month to bring out all the festivals *retained in our Calendar* both in red and black, for the month. At the end of the year this would make a thick volume.[5]

Newman offered to help the project by providing verse translations of the office hymns and presumably by being available for advice, and on 15 February Williams wrote:

> Wood and I are not a little pleased to find you have time to help us with our work on a point which we expected to give us some trouble. We were proposing to give the Hymns in Latin, with a running prose translation, for want of a better. We are taking the Roman order, so Wm.'s [Isaac Williams] translations will not

> interfere with yours, which we should prefer to have, if you did not object.[6] We have proposed to spend Easter at Oxford when we shall have much to consult you about. Our present wish for selection is to follow our own Calendar both black and red letter days, which on the whole does pretty well though it puts in occasionally what we should otherwise leave out, and, what is more annoying, compels us to omit some services, which we particularly wish to retain. One such we *must* retain, Dec 29 St. Thomas of Canterbury. Will Easter be sufficient time for you to receive the list of hymns, which we want, or shall we send them to you at once?[7]

Newman must have replied 'at once': Williams wrote on 18 February:

> The hymns that we want first are those of the 'Psaltery' and the 'Commons'. Most, if not all, of the former you have done, I believe, in No.75 of the Tracts, which we should like to adopt, if you did not feel that it was throwing our undertaking too much into connection with the Tracts, and so involving you, more than would be prudent, with the responsibility. If you thought so – we must adopt another version -- though after all the responsibility is only to the faithfulness of the translation – for which Wood is answerable.[8]

A few days later Newman heard from Wood:

> Robt. Williams has told you that it is the *Roman* Breviary we are taking. Truly it wd. have been a great piece of Anglicanismus to have taken the Paris one. What a real living connection have we with that place to tempt us to leave the Mistress of the world, the Mother of our churches, and not claim our filial share in her treasures? By the way, I wish you would get Isaac Williams to omit in His Collected Translations some remarks he every now and then goes out of his way to make on the variations between the two Breviaries: they really are merely formal ones. I am very glad indeed he is republishing; they will open the way for us, and not being *complete*, ours will still be wanted for *use* just as much. Have you already composed any of the hymns, or when do you think you will do so? I ask not as impatiently, nor as not fully feeling that our time must wait for yours, but merely because we should (for *our own convenience*) make arrangements for printing the Psaltery and Commons about June, if the Hymns were to be ready then, which will be wanted for the part. I think I have hit on what will be the

> best plan about the Proprium de Tempore; and that is to print it entire, but not to bring it out monthly, but altogether at the end of the next Church-year, to bind up with the Saints days which will then be complete. What do you say to this? I have just done the Commons, and will bring them down at Easter for you to glance over.[9]

Work continued on the translation and Newman contributed translations of the office hymns. On 23 March he was able to report to Wood, 'I am glad to tell you I am getting on very fairly with the translations of the Hymns.'[10]

Newman worked quickly at the translation of the Breviary hymns. He entered his translations, together with the date when each was completed, into two bound notebooks, and from these his progress can be traced. (See Chapter Eight.) He began with the hymns required for the Psalter; six of these were already translated in Tract 75. Another he had translated in March 1837. The remaining nineteen hymns he translated systematically between 18 February and 14 April 1838.

In May 1838 he translated the first twenty-four lines of *Stabat Mater dolorosa* (Vespers, Seven Sorrows of B.V.M., Friday after Passion Sunday) and *Tristes erant apostoli* (Vespers, common of apostles in Paschaltide). He resumed work in September and October 1838. Proper hymns were now required for the *Pars Hiemalis*, which the translators were hoping to publish by Easter 1839. He slightly revised his three Advent hymns from Tract 75 and made new translations of eight hymns for Christmas, Holy Innocents, Epiphany and Lent. He discontinued his translations when the project was abandoned towards the end of the year.

The translators fell behind with the schedule they had set themselves, as Williams wrote to Newman on 10 May:

> If you are now hurrying yourself with the hymns under the idea that we shall be in want of them soon, it is but fair to tell you that we have great doubt of being able to put our M.S.S. into sufficient state of accuracy to begin the printing just yet. Very many points we shall of course have to consult you upon, when we see you at Oxford,

> which must now be put off till Whitsuntide – but the great difficulty will be to secure the rendering the same expressions in emphasis by the same words in English and this will only be secured by allowing time for ourselves to get as familiar with the translation as with the original. Anyhow, you need not hurry yourself with the hymns, unless you like to get them off your hands – but we shall not want them immediately.[11]

An undated letter from Williams to Newman, written at about this time, refers to the decision of the translators to abandon the principle of a selective translation in accordance with the Calendar of the Book of Common Prayer:

> I believe Wood has told you of our determination, subject to whatever you may have to say about it, to make no selection, but print the whole Breviary – as at present used by the R. Cath.'s of England. He tells me that you wd write to me if you had any objections to make, and none having arisen I conclude you acquiesce. I believe this will not materially, if at all, encumber your labour in the Hymns.
>
> We find that the printing arrangements, paging etc., besides other reasons, will make it necessary to begin with the Pars Hiemalis Proprium, which together with the Psalter, we hope to bring out by Xmas at latest, if not by Advent; we should be glad therefore to have the Hymns of that quarter by the middle of October when we shall both be in London, and shall commence printing forthwith, and those of the Pars Verna not long after as that ought to be out by Feb 13 – Ash Wednesday. What would your experience of printing lead you to say of the possibility of passing through the press and publishing the Psalter and the Pars Hiemalis Proprium between the middle of October and Dec. 2 Advent Sunday? I fear the correction of the proofs will be a very long work, to get all the references, red letters etc. quite correct, which will be important.[12]

In Tract 75 Newman had shown considerable enthusiasm for the Roman Breviary and had recommended some use of it by his fellow Anglicans. The idea of a translation doubtless appealed to him. But he had almost certainly expressed caution about the advisability of publishing a translation. He also had reservations about his own involvement, or his apparent involvement, in it.

Wood and Williams were laymen and younger than Newman. Uninformed critics would be likely to hold Newman personally responsible for the project in general and for objectionable elements in the Breviary itself. The difficulties which Newman had foreseen soon manifested themselves. Strong criticism came from quarters hostile to the Tractarians, and, to Newman's sorrow, the project provoked sharp disagreement among his friends.

Meanwhile Robert Williams had evidently made himself objectionable again, for on 9 August Wood wrote to Newman:

> I have been a long while without writing to you, but I did not neglect the kind note you sent me on leaving town also its continuation concerning R.W. with whom I remonstrated; but I wish you, Breslin and others would row him on the spot for such outbreaks ...[13]

Wood also wrote about the objections already being made to the project and to his wish not to make it appear that Newman was totally associated with it, for Newman added a postscript to his reply of 23 August:

> As to the Breviary, is not this the way? whether people believe it or not, say in the Preface what is the fact that a friend has given you leave to use his translations and is not answerable for any thing. In this way I am clear of all but the abstract idea of translating from the Breviary Services. I think translating *all*, will diminish the attack on you from Protestants, as including the legends on Saints Days.[14]

Robert Williams was beginning to have doubts about the project because of growing opposition, and Newman was asked by Pusey:

> Will you caution Williams ... about the Breviary, as far as you think right; your extracts [Tract 75] have been the subject of a great deal of attack here, in part from what you say, in part from what you do not.[15]

John Keble had also been expressing misgivings, to judge from a letter Williams wrote to Newman on 30 August:

When I got to your letter I was writing for you a sketch of an Advertisement, and I have gone on with it, as you might like to show or tell Keble exactly with what view (so far as it can be stated extrinsically) we propose to publish. If we do end in doing so, I am quite sure it ought to be an Advertisement not a Preface.

But to get to the main subject: My view shortly is, and it is what has made me give the pains to it I have, that for the *good of the Church*, as a thing which will Catholicise our friends in all ways, the Breviary ought to be translated. The longer it is put off the more row it will make that is plain: it wd. have come out more quietly 2 years ago, and so on. Now if this is true, ought we to give it up against our own judgment that it is for the good of the Church, at the wish of persons who start on a different bottom; i.e. who wd. not enlarge the Reformation basis if they cd.? This seems to be the ground on which it ought to be put: is it more for the good of our Church that it shd. come out or no? If it seems that any split or protest among our friends (if it occur) will do more harm than the counterbalancing good, de Breviariis conclamatum est. But on this point I would like to put myself entirely into your hands; you must be much better able to judge. As to one's personal wishes, perhaps giving pain to one worthy person ought to outweigh them. I really think I look forward to as much annoyance as pleasure to myself if the thing goes on. Till we hear what Keble says on the whole matter, [if] any suggestion should strike you, I trust you will not fail to enlighten our inexperience in such matters therewith. Do you think Rivington the best person to employ?[16]

Meanwhile Newman's diary recorded continued activity with proofs passing between Williams and Newman.[17] Three extant letters [18] from Williams to Newman show the work still in progress in October 1838:

October 6. We are making a beginning of our printing. I fear the expense will oblige us to give up the red letters; and the expense is not the only objection, the time it would take and the blunders it would be liable to will probably determine us against it.

Will you please give me the corrections I have marked on the enclosed paper.[19] The third verse of the Hymn on Tuesday at Lauds, Wood wanted you to alter in some way, and I have never had it. I forget how I came to miss the other words; some I believe were torn off; some I could not read etc.

Also it would be a great convenience to us to know how many

hymns you would refuse to versify. Are they in the Proprium? and how would you propose that the unversified translations should be printed? with the original or without? Is it not rather essential that *Hymns* should be in *verse*? and would it not be better to give the original, when we had not an English versified translation, firstly a prosaic translation, arranged in lines, either in a footnote, or following the hymn in the text?

It is essential that I should have the words which are wanting in the Hymns immediately, as I shall be sending them to the press in a day or two. I hope it will not give you great inconvenience to let me have them.

We shall be able easily to pass the whole of the Pars Hiemalis with the Psalter through the press before Xmas – if we adopt the black only – will the hymns be ready for us? though I hate pressing you for them.

[postscript] What number of copies would you strike off?

October 15. Very many thanks for the Advent to Xmas Hymns – also, for what are coming. The printers assure me that we shall be able easily to put out all the Winter Proper before Xmas.

You will get this at Oxford, from whence you will send me the bits I want of the Hymns. I am sorry to trouble you, and hope it is not by any carelessness of mine that I am obliged to do so. Wood particularly wishes that we should quote the hymns by their initial English words, and it is, I suppose, better to do so. In order to do this, I must ask you for the initial words of the following Hymns, which occur (in the one vol. arrangement) in the Lauds of Sunday, in our first sheet.

Advent. En clara vox. this you have sent.

Lent. O Sol salutis. 1st Sunday in Lent. Lauds.

Passiontide Lustra sex. Passion Sunday. Lauds.

Easter. Aurora caelum purpurat. Low Sunday. Lauds. It is only the initial words I want, for quotation. Can you let me have these and the bits by Friday morning at latest? Wood closes with your very kind proposal to versify all the Hymns in your own way, and so do I, cordially. I think it gets us out of a great difficulty, for I could not bear the thought of a mere prose for what we called a *Hymn*. We shall probably give no footnotes – but merely say in the preface 'a friend has supplied us with translations of the Hymns, which are more or less literal etc.' – then put *all* the original Hymns in the appendix, and leave the intelligent reader to find out where the literal sense of anyone fails.

I shall be sorry if these Hymns should be a bother to you, with all your other work. Tho' it is perhaps of *some* consequence that the parts should come out before each Season commences, yet we will give up this, rather than you should be too hard pushed. It is unfortunate that Easter falls so early next year, which gives us a month less for each part than any other year we should have had. Ash Wednesday Feb. 13! We shall cut our Xmas holydays [sic] very short, to get the Spring Quarter out in time if possible . . .

I send you a specimen page, thinking you may like to see it. I have sent copy enough for the first sheet to the press, leaving spaces for initial words of the above Hymns, which will be ready for us on Friday – by which day Wood will be here, and I shall be returned from Dorset, where I go tonight.

We seem to have fixed upon 750 copies, unless you have any suggestions to make about this no . . .

October 23. We have arranged that each sheet of the proof shall be sent to you, in order that you can make any suggestions that occur to you, as well as correct the Hymns. You will return them regularly by return of post, that there may be no delay.

Among the doxologies sent that at Matins in Advent is omitted; will you supply it?

You will see us advertised to a great extent in a day or two.

[postscript] We will attend to all your wishes in the Preface.

Meanwhile the disagreement among Newman's friends was sharpening, and the objections tended to be levelled at Newman rather than at Wood and Williams. The opposition was led by Tom Keble, Isaac Williams and George Prevost. Tom Keble and Newman disagreed about the significance of the reformers of the sixteenth century. John Keble and Newman had both become rather critical of them, partly under the influence of Hurrell Froude. Tom Keble and Prevost, however, considered Newman and John Keble wrong to be so critical. 'I have been horrifying Newman with my Protestantism,' Tom wrote to his brother after a visit by Newman to Bisley.[20]

The opposition of Isaac Williams, Newman's curate until the previous year,[21] was in some respects surprising, especially as he had known and admired the Parisian Breviary since 1829 and had translated several of the hymns, some of which were later published.[22] He also admired Newman and enjoyed a close friendship with him. However, he also had a long-standing loyalty to the Kebles dating from his undergraduate days. He had first met John Keble in 1822 and had spent the next two summers reading under his tutorship at Southrop near Fairford, with Hurrell Froude and Wilberforce as fellow students. He owed much to the influence of the Kebles and had a great admiration for Bisley which was regarded by some of the early Tractarians as the ideal parish. Ordained deacon in 1829, Williams served his title at Windrush-cum-Sherborne, within reach of both Bisley and Fairford. He renewed his links with Tom Keble and Bisley on leaving Oxford in 1842.[23]

Although he was an enthusiastic Tractarian, writing Tracts 80 and 87 on 'reserve' and 86 on the Prayer Book, it was to be expected that his attachment to Tom Keble would lead him to side with him against Newman. Nor is it surprising if he was influenced by his brother-in-law George Prevost. Indeed it was Isaac Williams who coined the name 'the Bisley School' to designate himself, Tom Keble, George Prevost and their associates.[24] He does not make it explicit in his *Autobiography* why he was opposed to the project. Probably his main objection was that of the Bisley school, namely that it would have a Romanising influence.

George Prevost first met Isaac Williams as a fellow student at Southrop and he married Isaac's sister, Jane, in 1828. He served as curate to Tom Keble at Bisley 1828–34. He was also a keen Tractarian at that time,[25] although his only contribution to the Tracts was to complete Tract 84 (by Tom Keble) from page 35 onwards. Like Isaac Williams he felt a great loyalty to the Kebles, especially to Tom. He held a *via media* position regarding the Church of England. He found no difficulty in accommodating the Reformation and the work of the English reformers into his Catholic view of the Church of England: hence his disquiet at the Breviary project and his support for the Bisley school viewpoint.

Elizabeth Keble lived with her brother John at Hursley, but paid long visits to Tom at Bisley. It may have been during one of these visits that she read Tract 75, for she wrote an undated letter to John in which she mentioned it:

> I dare say you have looked at that Tract of Mr. N's about the Breviary. How much opposed he seems there to all the additions which he says were made by the Romanists of later times – As far as I have gone in Fleury there is nothing like the later ideas abt. the B.V. I cant help much laughter at the idea of my talking to you as if I knew anything worth telling thee.[26]

The letter suggests that she took more notice of Newman's criticisms of the Roman Breviary than of his praise of it. She happened to be at Bisley when she first heard of the translation project. It would seem that George Prevost, who was given to forthright talk, had been strongly criticising the project. His denunciation evidently made a strong impression on her for she immediately wrote to John on 30 October urging him to oppose the idea:

> . . . last night . . . the Prevosts, Mr Jeffreys and Mr. Rt. Barker were here at All Saints. . . . There was an intense discussion going on – Sir G Prevost being very seriously annoyed at the Publication of the translation of some Breviary I believe (by Mr. Wood and Williams) with prayers to the Virgin etc. – and from what they said it seemed to our poor judgements as well as theirs that if it could be [stopped (?)]. To me it ought to be suppressed. It must do so much harm and throw back many people who are . . .[27] opinion, besides encouraging the want of confidence which some people are beginning to have in Mr Newman. What can be the use of laying temptation in the way of people? Charles [28] you could hinder such things if you were to remonstrate, I am sure, and [you] are a better judge about them than Mr. N if you will but use your own judgment. You will be amused at this long piece of advice of mine but I was so haunted by it last night that I must pour it all out upon you – Sir G has written to Mr. Newman this morning so perhaps he will try to stop it. Mr. Jeffreys says he (Mr. N) defers to the opinion of young men too much and is too flattering to them and makes them have too high an opinion of themselves, and that Mr. Williams and Mr. Wood ought to be made to know their place. I hope you will take some notice of this petition and say what you think. My idea is from what I have heard that these two Mr. W's are less to be trusted than any of the party. Certainly if you and Mr. N do not disclaim having anything to do with the scheme it will be supposed and justly that you sanction it. Did not you tell me that Mr. Wood was being much inclined to be a Roman?

Later in the letter she showed how much she sided with Prevost and her brother Tom regarding the sixteenth-century reformers. She probably in addition disapproved of Hurrell Froude's *Remains*.

> What have you done about the other Vols. of Mr Froude's?[29] You do not mean that from your great dislike of the Reformers, and the way in which the Reformation was managed that you would like to go back to Romanism do you? and that you cannot excuse the Reformers or speak so tenderly of them as many people do. Dr. Pusey speaks very gently of it in that Preface to the Catena.[30] I suppose the difference is that you and Mr. N are more angry with them and he is more inclined to smoothe over it all.[31]

John did not reply to his sister's letter until 14 November. His letter is interesting as it shows that an alternative proposal was under active consideration, namely to publish a translation with certain omissions, such as feasts not in the Prayer Book Calendar, devotions to the Virgin Mary, invocation of the saints, and spurious hagiographical lessons at Matins, especially those replete with incredible miracles. John was not against an edited version of the Breviary, but he tried to persuade Newman to put an end to the project altogether because of the difficulty of deciding what to expurgate. He also explains his exact position regarding the sixteenth-century reformers.

> I think the translation of the whole Breviary, except as a document, clearly wrong, and have written to N. to say so: because it seems to me trifling with holy things, and disrespectful to those to whom we wish to have respect: in short against such texts as 'See thou do it not' etc. But I do not see how the same objection holds against an *expurgated* edition of it in English: although I clearly see that the Expurgator incurs a very heavy responsibility, and partly on that account and partly to satisfy such as Prevost, I rather advised N. in a second letter to suspend the printing for a time; but he had committed himself before my second letter came. As to the Reformers, I certainly do think that *as a set* they belonged to the same class with the Puritans and Radicals, and I have very little doubt that if we had lived in those times neither my Father nor you nor Prevost nor Harrison would have had anything to do with

> them. And I think we shall never be able to make our ground good against either Romanists or Puritans till we have separated ourselves and our Liturgy from them. But this is a very different thing from trying to change the Liturgy as we have it. The case corresponds to that of the Revolution in politics.[32]

John Keble was in accord on most matters with Newman, but on this issue he had grave misgivings. He, like Newman, ardently desired to maintain concord among the members of the movement and found himself in some difficulty because of his close ties to his brother and the 'Bisley school' and the affection and loyalty he felt for Newman. He also, like Newman, found himself caught in the mid-ground of the cross-fire and compelled to play an uncongenial role as peacemaker. He likewise shared Newman's distaste for acting as final arbiter, even though Newman would willingly have followed his advice as the dispute dragged on. But John Keble would not give him directive guidance.

Matters came to a head at the beginning of November when Prevost wrote a brief letter to Newman on 2 November 1838.

> Every body, whom I have yet seen, of those who used to sympathise with us, is greatly distressed at the intended publication of this translation of the Roman Breviary –
>
> If the authors could be persuaded on our earnest entreaty to suppress it, I will be ready to be answerable for all the expense incurred thereby.
>
> Only please to write to me word as soon as possible whether this request (which I write with the entire concurrence of [T.] Keble and Jeffreys) can be complied with.[33]

Newman took offence at what he considered to be a peremptory demand and replied on the following day:

> I at first intended to do what doubtless you meant me to do – to convey your letter to the Translators and Editors of the Breviary. You must have wished me to do so, because the simple reason you use against their undertaking is that you and others dislike it. This, I feel, to be a strong one – but it could not weigh with persons, till they knew who the parties were.

But when I came to think, I determined to wait for a second letter from you for this reason – because I feel sure that the one I have received will appear to strangers peremptory. It would give me greater satisfaction in informing the parties in question of your wishes, if they had not been conveyed with the request to return an answer 'as soon as possible'. This will appear to strangers like summoning a town to capitulate. Depend upon it, such a course is not persuasive. You say you write in a hurry, which doubtless accounts for your *apparently* abrupt and positive tonc.[34]

To this Prevost replied at greater length and apologetically on 7 November:

I am very sorry that I should have seemed to have written in a peremptory or uncourteous manner. . . . I never thought of my letter being forwarded to the Editors, but rather that you should understand it as a request for you to communicate the proposal if you thought good . . . Indeed if you knew in how much distress of mind I, or (I might say) we wrote that letter, I do not think you would take our expressions much amiss . . .[35]

Meanwhile J. W. Bowden wrote to Newman on 5 November:

I find that Wood and Williams have changed their plans and are going to publish the *whole* Breviary – is not this wrong? – taking into view their way of talking about it, I cannot but rather fear for the consequences – the issue of fact, as it seems to me, between your friends and their impugners is, whether you are leading them to what Rome is or to what Rome was . . . I dislike the connection of your name with it, thro' the hymns – I suppose you will cause them to insert, in their preface, a disclaimer of any general responsibility of yours for publication – I wish instead of the present Breviary, they had thought of something in use in ante-Tridentine times – some MS. of the Use of Sarum etc . . .[36]

In reply Newman wrote to Bowden on 6 November, reiterating his position on the project:

I am sure I wish the Breviary done in the best way. W. and W. are not to commit me, stating in the Preface etc. Dr. Rock, Lord

> Shewsbury's Chaplain, tells us that the R.C.'s in England *are about to* adopt the Sarum Breviary . . .[37]

On the same day Newman wrote to Keble, anxious for his guidance:

> On Saturday morning I had a letter from Prevost, protesting in strong terms against the Breviary being published. I wished to send it to Wood and Williams but felt that some explanation was necessary to send them so needlessly abrupt a letter. Wood sends me back the answer I inclose, which you will see, implies (what I had told him) that though I did not feel that Prevost's opposition was an insurmountable objection, I would translate no more hymns without your leave. Your letter has saved me the awkwardness of writing to you on the subject. What I proposed to Wood was to correct the Breviary by *some standard*. I confess I much dislike correcting it by my private judgment or the vague opinions of the day, or by 'what people will think'. I mentioned to him the 39 Articles – calling it 'The Breviary reformed according to 39 Articles' I do not see that his objection is a good one – but *this* seems a strong one, viz. the 39 Articles would not cut out the Legends. Then I thought of the Preface to the Prayer Book. What would you say to 'according to both together'? – But after all is there any of our standards which would cut out such as the following: 'Let St. Mary and all Saints intercede for us to the Lord, etc., that we may be worthy to be aided and saved by Him who liveth etc.'? Are we bound to cut out what is of unknown antiquity and not forbidden by our Church?
>
> Of course the sooner I can have your answer conveniently to yourself the better. They go printing on, but this at present will involve very little cancelling, for scarcely more than the 'Ave Maria' occurs in the Psalter which they are doing . . . [Footnote] I do not think it will do to attempt to correct it by *history*. None of the parties concerned are strong enough in facts to do so.[38]

After writing this, Newman received a further letter from Wood, written on 6 November, proposing that Newman should decide on certain omissions to be made from the translation to 'bring it into harmony with the English Church' and to make this clear in a preface:

> Since my hurried note of last night an idea has occurred to me,

which, in case of Keble's giving judgement against the entire Breviary coming out, I should wish you to have without delay.

Robert Williams's repugnance to undertaking any retrenchment *himself* is so strong that this is out of the question; and my own opinion is as decided as to the impropriety of a young layman's doing it. But *if you and I wish it*, he will agree to devote the time and money which has been and has to be expended on it to such an expurgate Edition undertaken by a person who likes and feels competent to make the omissions. In other words, if you will write a Preface with your name or initials saying that some friends of yours have put a Translation of the Breviary into your hands, and that you have undertaken to give it to the world with such omissions as bring it into harmony with the English Church, he will go on with me translating, preparing and correcting for the press, and bearing the expense. Now under the circumstances I think I may say I *do* wish this very much, and it does not at first sight seem to involve you in any more than No. 75 has already. All the *trouble* you need have about it, will be the Preface, which may be as short as you like, and deciding on the omissions. You may say that your friends have undertaken all mechanical labor, and so not be answerable for blunders. In this case we would send you the Psalter in sheets, to direct what cancels need be made, (I don't think if the initial Hail Mary etc is cancelled, the references need be) and then as each proof of the Proprium came out you should have it to omit or modify. Long before the Proprium was out, you would make up your mind what course to pursue as to the Saints days, and direct us accordingly.

Should you like this, and it proceed well, all that has happened may bring out more good, and so bring a greater blessing on all of us . . .

It will be well, if only as regards the Printers, to decide as soon as may be.[39]

Such was the speed of the post that Newman received this letter on the same day that it had been written, and that evening he forwarded Wood's letter to Keble, adding on the top of it:

I have just received this, and am disposed to think that, if they sacrifice their plan to me, they have some call on me to do what they here suggest.[40]

This crossed in the post with a letter from Keble dated 7

November in which he sympathised both with Newman and the 'Bisley school'. He was mildly critical of Williams and Wood, but recognised their good intentions. Above all he endeavoured to make peace and advocated suspending the project until the time was ripe for it:

> I feel that we are got rather into a difficulty owing to the overhasty proceedings of the two W's; though one feels the greatest respect for their motives and the energy with which they have undertaken this work, I cannot understand their not bearing the responsibility of selection when they are willing to bear that of the whole work . . . I confess, therefore, I could find it in my heart, considering the feelings of such people as Prevost, my brother, Harrison and Isaac Williams, to wish that their work might be suspended for the present . . . If however it is thought best under all circumstances to proceed, I do not see how they could do better than make their own corrections and submit them to you: the submission will take away whatever might be presumptuous in the effort as a *Lay* effort. And it seems to me that the best rule of correction would be to give themselves time to go through the matter historically: failing that, to take care to abide by the Articles and Liturgy *to which they are pledged*, and to err on the safe side, i.e. rather to leave out what you would wish to insert, then vice versa: taking care to announce in the Preface, that one is not to be understood as condemning all that one omits. The more I think on it, the more impossible it seems to me to be right in translating the whole . . . I think it rather hard that the whole burthen should be thrown upon you: but I suppose it is what in your position you must expect. Of course you will make use of me, if I can be of any use, in the revising. I think the Preface should take notice of the objection, 'Will not any book of the kind interfere with the Prayer Book?' . . .[41]

On the same day Newman wrote to Keble:

> I conceive that you will quite approve of Wood's proposal in his second letter – since it involves me in no greater responsibility than you consider I already incur, while it gives me control. So I have written to tell Wood that, *as so* conceiving, I will accept his offer . . .[42]

As a result of this agreement, Wood was able to write to Newman on 8 November in a happier vein:

I cannot tell you how rejoiced I am, *personally*, at your having undertaken to revise the Breviary; and the more I think of it the more satisfied I am that *under the circumstances* it is the best thing that could be done. If we could have been left to ourselves to bring the entire Breviary out quietly, and not have involved you in it at all, I still think this wd. have been best of all. But perhaps we have hitherto acted too much as a party to make this possible; and at any rate people do not seem to see the distinction between your giving Poetry to a ready-made plan, and actually co-operating in it, so you might have unawares committed yourself much more than you will now do. Still I quite sympathize in your not 'liking' what fate has forced upon you, and am very sorry for it. I shall console myself with setting down per contra the alleviation of William's disappointment; as for myself, I don't feel I deserve much credit for giving up.

And now for business: the whole printing is suspended, and I send you down partly in clean sheets, partly in proof what has been done up to now, that you may direct the cancels. It wd. be very nice if you would let me have them again on Saturday evening by coach, they had better come to Grosvenor Square. In Advent there will so little (as you know) to cancel, that I think we go on sending you it in proof to cancel, without any expense. When it comes (say) the Nativity, or parts which will involve Addresses to the Virgin, we will send you a Latin Brev. we have in sheets to mark with pencil or red ink what is to be omitted, previously; but you shall have the proofs also. (I still think mere referential words in the Psalter 'Hail Mary' might stand, or be obliterated with a black dab of ink.)

If we can thus proceed without much delay the first parts may still come out in Advent, and in the next Advertisement may be inserted something which might seem only to have been omitted for brevity's sake in the first. Then the world at large will know nothing of any change of plan. In this case, tell us what shd. be added implying selection etc; and also we shd. have the Preface in a fortnight's time: we will send all the *technical* details for it; and *now* you may refer fully to No. 75. [Crossed out by Wood: What do you think of printing the omittenda in Latin in the foot-notes?]

Our plan is to bring out *all* the Proprium de Tempore *first*, so you have 3 months or more to make up your mind about the Festa[43] in.

[Footnote:] Williams will not let you bear the Cancels, and I, as an unprejudiced party, decide against the propriety of you doing so.[44]

On 10 November Williams wrote apologetically to Newman, who copied parts of the letter to Keble:[45]

Wood is particularly busy with Education matters, and has asked me to write what we have to say in answer to your communication of today, which I am the more ready to do as I have confessions to make and sorrow to express for the rash talking which Mr. Keble speaks of. I have only to *mend* for the future; for the past pain I have given him and other friends, I will beg you, if you will, to express my sorrow.

I am disappointed at the decision against immediate publication, but we both acquiesce, as in duty bound; on the question of the *printing*, however, there are circumstances which oblige us to say that it must be *now*, if at all,

Not only should we find it impossible to lay aside all our work, and, after turning to other pursuits, be sure of having time on our hands to resume it at any future time, but our engagements are such with the printers that we must either proceed with the work, or offer them some large remuneration for the expense that they have incurred on the faith of our proceeding with it. They have had an extra new type, including those V/'s and R/'s, cast expressly for this work, for which they would require a considerable remuneration. It is clear then that the printing must proceed, as it seems Mr. Keble is not adverse to its appearing at some future time.

As the book is not to be published now, I think there will be no need to trouble you at the present time to proceed with your cancels. All the proofs which you would be likely to cancel are already printed off, and nothing can occur of an objectionable nature in the Proprium. If you will continue to supply versified translations of such hymns as you approve, we will go on as originally proposed, not troubling you about those hymns which you had intended to have modified; this plan we had rather adopt than any other, fully confident that on further consideration the entire publication will be preferred to a garbled one; but be that as it may be, we shall leave the sheets wholly in your power to do what you like with, and I promise to bear the expense of such cancels as you wish to make, if any, whenever you take upon yourself the Editorship of it.

We will wait for your leave to proceed thus, which we hope you will not withhold, that we may recommence on Monday morning. And will you direct your letter to Wood, 36 Grosvenor Square, not under cover to me – as my letters all go into the city. If you can, do palliate my foolish and rash talking, which is what *I* will not attempt; and if I have caused pain to any, ask them to forgive me.[46]

Newman evidently did not entirely agree, and Williams wrote another submissive letter on November 13:

I have first to say that we fully see the force of your objections to our proposed plan, and agree that only whatever is to be eventually published must be now printed. We are therefore in your hands, and will obey your orders punctually whatever they may be.

But before we proceed to the printing an altered version, I wish to say something on two points.

The first relates to an expression, underlined as if it contained the gist of this objection, in a letter of Wilson's which speaks of Mr. Keble's views.

The second point relates to a few of the difficulties in the way of making omissions, which have occurred to us, worth considering, and to which you will have to direct your attention before you begin.

1. The expression in Wilson's letter is 'as a *devotional book*'. Now, for my own part, I can truly say that I have always considered that as laymen (and indeed as individuals, even though we had been clerics) we had no authority, or personal intentions, to take upon ourselves the responsibility of putting out a book of devotion. In whatever I have said on the subject I have all along grounded my apology on this – that I was *not* putting forth a book of devotion – my wish has always been to say in our preface, if we had one, 'we are two laymen, taking upon ourselves no responsibility but the fidelity of the translation, leaving to people to use this book as they see fit, on their own responsibility – those who can read Latin can now so use it, and can buy a copy in any shop, all we do is to put those who cannot read Latin into the same position.' In my own mind, there have been several uses to which I have thought it might and could be put, but to each, in the responsibility of those who use it; and I should have had no objection to enumerate some in the preface, if it had been specially wished, but I should *not* have enumerated them, if left to myself. These various purposes are such as their devotion, first, of course; a help to judge of the ethos of the Reformation; a help also to judge of the ethos of the Roman Ch. as compared with antiquity; and, as respects the Legends, a remonstrance with that Ch. against taxing so severely the faith of Xns etc etc etc. To all these purposes the Breviary is clearly applicable by those who like so to use it, and our own translation, if *literally faithful*, would only help people to apply it – Now, do you think the objections of people to a *literal* version would be answered by its being preceded by a preface of this sort? – Will you take sufficient time to consider, and to consult others upon this point? I do not say this out of any desire to open the original question, if that question has been understood, but from a suspicion that the objections turn

upon its being put out *as a devotional book*, and to such objections, I own, *I* should give weight, indeed have felt them all along.

My second point relates to the difficulties of selection. The objectionable passages are of two sorts. Those in the Festa are long legends, which must be wholly omitted; and so all mention of that Saint omitted; and so a new Calendar formed, which will be neither Roman, nor our own, for the subject matter of festivals that occur in our own Calendar is as objectionable as that of any others; such a Calendar in fact would be formed either by taking the credulousness of the compilers' own mind as the proper standard, or by boldly rejecting all supernatural events since the apostles' days as untrue. – The other class of objectionable passages are those which occur in the midst of other matter, high expressions etc., but expressions and thoughts which more or less go to make up the ethos of the whole. How to deal with either satisfactorily passes my comprehension, I own; but I have no doubt that, if you undertake it, you will surmount these difficulties – and again I have to respect that we are *wholly in your hands*. Do not trouble yourself to answer this before you have made up your mind as to the course to be pursued *throughout* not only the Psalter and Proprium, but also the Commons and Festa; and then we will be your hands and eyes, at command, till the work is complete.

It is but fair to say that Wood does not feel with me the objection of putting it out entire as *a devotional book*;[47] he would wish to do so, but would no doubt acquiesce in *any* preface that would satisfy our friends – and I suggest one, as above, which accords with my views of our position.[48]

On 16 November Williams wrote again:

As soon as we begin again, we shall want either the whole or the initial words of the hymn Exultet orbis gaudiis, on S. John's day. Either will do, so if you cannot supply it entire, we can easily refer to it in the Common of Apostles.

We are anxiously looking for your answer, being wholly at a stand, till we receive it; from the delay I augur well, as a proof that at least you have not thought the proposition to our friends of publishing the whole as a mere document, altogether hopeless.

It is perhaps worth your knowing, that all the persons to whom I have mentioned this question, not only now, but all through the past year, I mean, particularly those who do not feel with you on Church matters, have been strong in advising an *entire* publication,

> as the only course that can save us from responsibility; and generally they advise no preface, though they ask for a statement concerning the 'errors of Popery'. This we should give them by quoting the articles.[49]

Newman made the position clear to Keble in a letter of 17 November, to which he attached an extract from Williams's letter of 10 November:

> On receipt of your last I wrote at once to W. and W., undoing what I had done, and stopping the cancelling etc. What Williams says I will extract. However, he begged very hard to be allowed to go on printing, on the full understanding that I was to have entire command over its publication and the direction of all cancels and alterations – on the grounds that they had made engagements with a printer, ordered new type, etc., and would incur a most considerable expense for nothing unless they printed now. On these considerations and conditions I allowed as much as this. But the publication of course is absolutely suspended . . .[50]

However, when Williams and Wood realised a few days later the extent and character of the revision which Newman proposed should be made to the translation, they decided to abandon the project entirely. As his letters to Keble show, Newman had considered various ways of modifying the translation to make it acceptable to Anglicans generally, but he had found it impossible to please everybody. Instead he received constant criticism, to which perhaps he was over-sensitive. There were repeated requests to alter the translation or to stop the project entirely. The document setting out Newman's proposed alterations has not survived. It is possible that his revision was over-cautious.

Williams and Wood decided to abandon the translation firstly because the modifications proposed by Newman went far beyond anything they had anticipated. Already disappointed at the difficulties encountered in carrying out their original project in its entirety, they were not prepared to see their cherished project further diminished. Secondly, they desired to spare Newman further disquietude. To go on any further would involve themselves and Newman in a version of the Breviary with which none of them would be satisfied. Wood accordingly wrote to Newman on 20 November:

> I am very glad that you have sent us these specimens of the way in which you would modify the Breviary, as it enables us to realise it more than we had before done. What occurs to both of us upon it is this: 1st. that it will take up a great deal more of your *time and thoughts* than it is fair to do upon the mere *contingency* of a future publication: 2nd. as to the alterations themselves; I must tell you honestly we don't like them, and should be unwilling to see you hastily committed to them . . .
>
> These determinations have made us determine to suspend the printing for the present altogether, and to pay off the printer as if we had done with him, and to lay our clean sheets upon a shelf. Should the day come when the whole Breviary is called for as a Document or otherwise we may take up our work where we left off . . .
>
> And now . . . you must let me tell you my dear Newman how very sensible we have been of your tender kindness towards us, and which has been no small consolation under the feeling that others would be thinking us rash and self-willed . . .
>
> I should tell you why we do not (at first sight) like your suggested emendations; it is chiefly that they are not mere omissions, but substitutions; perhaps one might do this not to leave a service incomplete by a single antiphon, but to do it in extenso – surely one great part of the Breviary is that its forms have become sacramental . . .[51]

Newman doubtless felt some relief at their decision: relief that a source of anxiety had been taken away rather than relief that there was to be no translation. He conveyed the news to Keble with no comment except 'I think all persons should remember that they have done this at a pecuniary sacrifice, besides the disappointment.' The rest of the letter is taken up with a lengthy account of disagreements and misunderstandings, especially with Tom Keble and Prevost.[52] There had been difficulties and differences over the Tracts, the Library of the Fathers, and various articles, as well as over the Breviary translation. Newman seemed to take offence and feel hurt very readily. To Keble, and perhaps to no one else, he revealed a painful sensitivity to the attitudes and remarks of his friends. Two lengthy letters from Keble (26 November, 8 December) were taken up with explanation, reconciliation, reassurance and attempts to soothe his feelings.[53] In the first of these letters Keble remarked in parentheses: 'for you know, my dear N., you are a very sensitive person.'

If others seemed unaware of his sensitivity, it may have been because he veiled it with a certain hardness and severity. He was particularly disappointed that Frederic Rogers, his former pupil, the close friend who had urged him to accept Froude's Breviary, disagreed with him. In 1886 Rogers (then Lord Blachford) wrote to Anne Mozley about this when she was preparing Newman's letters for publication:

> March 5, 1886. Curiously enough I see by an old diary, under date December 12, an account of – I am at a loss for a substantive – not a quarrel, not exactly difference, but a kind of stern alienation for a fortnight, ending in tender reconciliation, which was due to this difference between himself as supporter of (S.) Wood, (R.) Williams, and Oakeley, who were pressing the publication of the 'Breviary' on one side, and T. Keble and Prevost on the other. I seem to have objected to some actual or intended letter to Keble, and I certainly in my mind, and probably in the tone of my conversation, sided on the whole with the Prevost side rather than with the Wood and Williams side. This made me a disagreeable confidant to him, and this again he took as very unkind, and showed it in a certain flinty way which he had at command on great emergencies. But then, you occasionally saw what this flintiness cost him. And when you came to frank explanation, there came from the rock a gush of overpowering tenderness.[54]

Even the gentle Isaac Williams noted a certain asperity which was otherwise not characteristic of Newman:

> The first secret misgiving which arose into something of distrust was when two of Newman's pupils – S. Wood, since dead, and Robert Williams (M.P. for Dorchester) – were translating and on the point of publishing the Roman Breviary (with the hymns translated by Newman) without any omissions. On Prevost's

> earnestly deprecating this, a dispute ensued, and I thought Newman showed some want of meakness. This, and not his opinions, weakened in some slight degree my confidence; and in looking back, most intimately as I was united with him, I cannot remember when my prayer for him was not rather that he might be preserved from error and the dangers to which he was exposed from his peculiar temperament, than for his perfection, and that I might follow his example, as would have been my prayer with regard to John Keble and Pusey. But it is only on the retrospect one is sensible of this difference.[55]

Doubtless Newman over-reacted, making too much of differences of opinion and taking offence unnecessarily. He was genuinely saddened to see his friends disunited, As he told Bowden:

> I am so bothered and attacked on all sides by friends and foes, that I had much rather say nothing . . . I mean, I distrust my judgment and am getting afraid to speak. It is just like walking on treacherous ice: one cannot say a thing but one offends someone or other . . . You cannot conceive what unpleasant tendencies to split are developing . . .[56]

His love for the Breviary was undiminished, but he could see the force of the objections raised against an unedited translation or any translation at all. He continued to recite the Breviary privately whenever he could. Whatever his hopes might have been that the Breviary could in some form be offered one day for the use of Anglicans, the translation project now seemed at a complete end.

CHAPTER FIVE

The Breviary Translation Project – Phases Two and Three

The project had ceased, but it was not forgotten. A letter from John Keble to Newman dated 7 September 1839 shows that the question of a translation was still under discussion. Keble wrote the letter when sending Newman his manuscript of the preface to the third volume of Froude's *Remains*:

> I hope I have not put you or the Printers out by this delay. The stuff I send you is poor and prosy enough, but if it does no good I hope it will do no harm to the Breviary, it requires in my mind a fuller explanation than I have had or can well conjecture, to alter materially the notion I had before. If it is to come out not as a document but as a Book of Devotion, it still seems to me disrespectful to God and His Saints, and uncharitable to many persons – I do not mean Protestants, but ill informed persons generally – to insert the Prayers which [we] ourselves think objectionable, without some express caution or warning. If it may be done with selection in the way I proposed when we were talking of it before, I should think it, myself, a very good thing. But I am a good deal apprehensive that [Williams (obliterated)] is either so wilful or so much under some bad guidance that neither step will add much to his security. I don't mean to speak harshly of him, for indeed I like him as everyone must extremely: but I think there is in him a want of submissiveness – a sort of great boy's way of taking things . . .[1]

The project was actively resumed by Williams in 1841. He was assisted by Samuel Wood and Frederick Oakeley. The venture also received warm support from Pusey at this stage. It was planned to incorporate the translations of the office hymns which Newman had composed for Tract 75 and to persuade him to provide further translations. In late June or early July 1841 Robert Williams wrote to Bloxam, who had been curate at Littlemore since 1837:

> I have determined to begin the Breviary without delay. It may perhaps be September before I begin printing, but I shall have a good deal at first, whilst I am in the country, anyhow I hope to get the Pars Hiemalis out by Advent. I can get no publisher to take it, and if I could, I should hardly consent, since I find it would nearly double the price. The expense moreover is rather more than I can comfortably afford, so I would take loans if you know of any persons willing to advance money for the purpose to be repaid when the work is sold, or at the end of a year at all events. I should need no money till January next, as Leslie will pay the printer till then. I hope Newman will let us have the hymns, and will do more. I have written to him on the subject, and hope you will do your best to persuade him . . .
>
> Will you please get me the introductions promised by Drs. Rock and Wiseman to someone I might consult in case of difficulty. I would have some conversation with him before I left town, which I shall do early in August.
>
> I suppose you would not advise taking a loan from the Roman Catholics. [postscript] I hope I shall get the price down to 8/– a volume, or at most 10/–.[2]

The project, however, was beset with problems. There was difficulty in finding a publisher and the cost was prohibitive. Oakeley wrote to Bloxam on 26 May:

> Robert Williams is dismayed at the cost of publishing his Translation of the Roman Breviary. No publisher will undertake the work. He wishes to know what chance there is of a subscription, and whether you think Mr. Ambrose Phillips, etc. will guarantee taking a good many copies? Do what you think best however, and talk to Ward . . .[3]

Negotiations were taking place with J. H. Parker at Oxford for publication on a subscription basis, but the proposed breviary would be expensive to set up in type and it was uncertain how well it would sell. Robert Williams wanted to sound out Roman Catholic reaction to the proposed translation, partly to ensure that the Roman Catholic authorities in England, and especially Wiseman, would not raise difficulties and oppose the publication, and also to determine how much interest there would be among Roman Catholics in buying copies. Williams did not want to get involved personally with Ambrose Phillipps or Wiseman, and had to persuade Oakeley or Ward to negotiate on his behalf and without mentioning his name. He also wanted an introduction to a Roman Catholic rubricist whom he could consult privately for advice. He discussed his problems in a letter to Bloxam on 4 June 1841:

> I am sorry to have delayed so long in answering your letter to Oakeley, which he gave me to answer before I went out of Town. I could not make up my mind what to do without a good deal of consideration. It strikes me that Phillipps' notion of my Translation of the Breviary being sold to Roman Catholics *for use in their chapels* must be absurd. I am glad to know he is interested in it, and probably we should find there would be a considerable sale amongst them, but I am of opinion this ought not to affect the *plan* of the work, the main object of which must be to influence *our own* people, and for that purpose we must use our own version etc. etc.
>
> I am quite prepared to undertake the Editorship of the work, if I have the assurance from some (Roman) Catholics of more consideration than Mr. Phillipps that such a work would not shock their feelings: and if any arrangement can be made with some Publisher to take all the risk and expense of the publication. I cannot induce Leslie to do so, but perhaps you could induce Parker to take it. He would be the best man on many accounts, and you could give him such an idea of the probable sale as to induce him to enter into it. It must be printed in London if *I* am to superintend the proofs, and by Messrs Lacy, Norton & Co. to whom I am under an obligation to offer it.
>
> The cost of printing, paper, for 750 copies may be estimated when I have printed the first sheets at about £500. These sheets must be cancelled, and it is decidedly my opinion that it must be printed in 4 volumes on the same arrangement as the original. This will make the expense greater then the sum above stated, besides which it is worth considering whether we should have an edition of 1000, instead of 750. It would be a great thing if the price could be

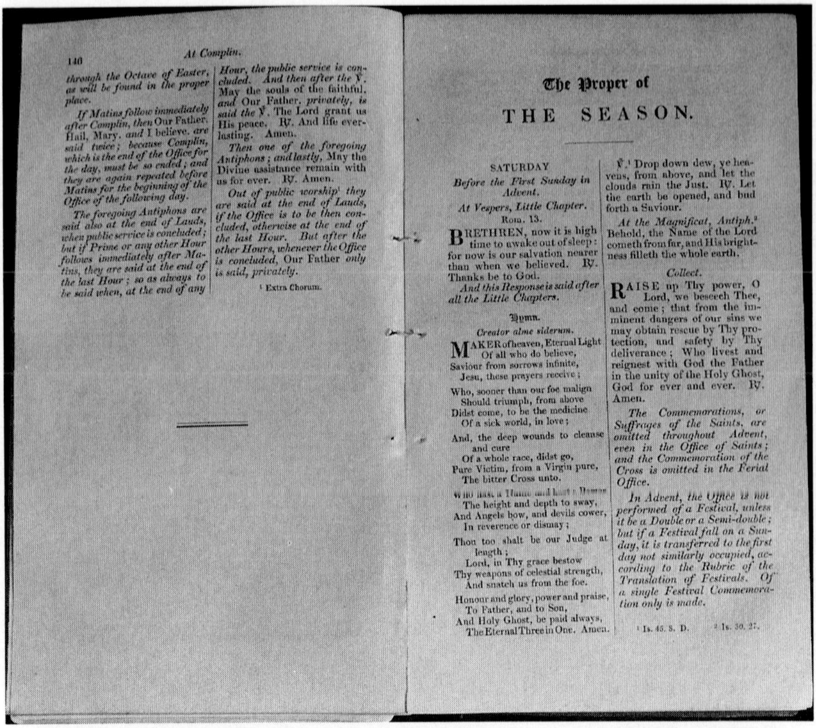

Plate 1 Fascicule of the translation of the Roman Breviary produced by Samuel Wood and Robert Williams. On the left is page 146, the final page of the Psalter. On the right is page 147, the beginning of the Proper for Advent. It includes Newman's translation of the hymn 'Creator alme siderum': 'Maker of heaven, Eternal Light'. (The first stanza of this translation was later altered.)

Plate 2 Newman's room at the Birmingham Oratory.

as low as £1.10.0 and it certainly would not be more than £2.0.0. We should make some stipulation of this sort with the Publisher. Should you mind going to Parker and making the proposal to him? Would you also write to Ambrose Phillipps and state my difficulty upon publishing such a work, without mentioning my name, and say that it can only be overcome by the assent of Dr. Wiseman and others of that communion to the plan. Is Dr. Rock in Phillipps' league? If not, I should like his opinion. Also if I undertake it I should like an introduction to some Ritualist, who would consent to give me such explanation as I might need of technical words in the rubric, and of the meaning of some rubrics.

You may assure Mr. Phillipps that he is welcome to as many copies of the Psalter as he likes. If you will send me his address I will forward him a dozen or more copies with some copies of the daily psalms, and the Penitential Psalms, and the Prayers following, which perhaps he will like to see – *as from you*.

I believe Oakeley is in Oxford. Will you show him this letter and talk to him about it, and remind him to bring up the copy of the Sarum Breviary, from which Seager is going to reprint, for me.[4]

I suppose Phillipps' observation upon the use of *red* letters applies to Sarum and not to the English Breviary. If so, I agree with him; but I think great care ought to be taken to keep down the price of the English Translation, as all its efficiency will depend upon its wide circulation, and the Red Letters will almost double the cost, but if a favourable pecuniary arrangement can be made with Parker, perhaps we might manage the Red. The advantages both in beauty and in clearness are very great.

Mr Phillipps ought certainly to be cautious in the use of the Psalter. But if I do engage in the work, since no one else will be responsible, I have no character for orthodoxy to lose! There need be no concealment about it. Till the arrangement is made, it had certainly better not be talked of.[5]

It is not certain whether Newman actually agreed to supply the hymn translations for this proposed translation. Williams seemed quite determined to go ahead, not only with the translation, but with a complete text and on a rather more ambitious scale than before. Whether he succeeded in reaching an agreement with Parker is not known. The practical obstacles, especially the expense, were considerable.

There were also, we may assume, the same religious objections as before. The Roman Breviary in its entirety was in

Anglican eyes a distinctively Roman Catholic book, and there were critics within the Tractarian circle as well as outside of features such as the Hail Mary and the invocation of saints. Furthermore there were difficulties in presenting the Breviary as part of the heritage of the Western church. The Breviary which Williams was translating was an edition published in the nineteenth century of the *Breviarium Romanum* as reformed and edited after the Council of Trent and authorised by Pius V in 1568, and subsequently amended by Clement VIII and Urban VIII. Although the only major difference between this breviary and a late medieval one was the hymns, which had been greatly changed by Urban VIII, it would appear to most Anglicans what it officially was, namely the divine office as currently authorised and published by the Roman Catholic authorities. Some of its features militated against the principles of the Reformation. If some of the Tractarians were sensitive to these issues, it can be imagined how hostile would 'Protestant' opinion be to the Roman Breviary.[6]

More plausible perhaps was the alternative plan sometimes mentioned of translating the Sarum Breviary, but even here there were difficulties. It was just as objectionable to 'reformed' belief as the Roman Breviary. Secondly, it had not undergone any revision in the sixteenth century and was still in its medieval form. Thirdly, the Church of England had officially abolished the use of the Sarum Breviary and the Roman Missal, and had replaced them with the Book of Common Prayer. It was difficult then to see what status the Breviary could have had among Anglicans, even as a work of private devotion.

To accept a major part of Roman Catholic liturgy without accepting the totality of Roman Catholic belief on the sacraments and the nature of the Eucharist, on which the liturgy rests, was a difficult step for many Anglicans. One can understand some of the misgivings held by Newman's friends: was it prudent to offer the Roman Breviary to Anglicans? Was there a danger of rushing things? Thoughts such as these doubtless lay behind Keble's characterisation of Wood and Williams as 'overhasty'.

One of the strongest ground of objection was the likely 'romanising' effect of the Breviary. Newman did not reveal to others that at that time the Breviary was beginning to have such an effect on himself. To his friends at this time he must have appeared inconsistent and enigmatic: loving the Breviary, yet seeking extensive deletions and amendments to avoid giving offence, and all the time holding back from giving unequivocal support to the translators. It seems that few of his associates knew the precise grounds of his reluctance to let the project go ahead. Bloxam was surely very close to the controversy, and in constant touch with the translators, and yet he regarded Newman's action as something of a mystery, which for him at least was not solved until 1867:

> Visiting some relations at Edgbaston near the Oratory in the Autumn of 1867, I started for the purpose of calling upon Newman on the 4th of September. As I reached the gate of the grounds he was passing by with Father Neville for the purpose of taking a walk. I joined them and in the course of conversation enquired why the Translation of the Roman Breviary had been stopped. He said it was done at the request of Keble. Knowing that the translation of the hymns in that portion of the Breviary, which had been printed, were his, I asked if he had translated any more of them, he replied that he had, and they appeared soon after in a volume of Poems published by him. Frederick Oakeley, then Fellow of Balliol, and Robert Williams, M.P. for Dorchester, undertook the general translation, and completed the seven services as far as the Fourth Sunday in Advent inclusive, 192 pages, when it was given up.[7]

Whether Newman meant by this that Keble had at last given him specific advice or that Keble requested Newman to stop the translation is not clear. The full correspondence between the two men on this stage of the project has not survived. Newman's letter to Keble on 23 July 1841 implied that he had independently made his own mind up:

> I have just stopped Robert Williams going on with the printing of the translation of the Breviary. He would not print it without my countenance, and that I did not feel I could *give*. But men *will* be doing something.[8]

This implication is even stronger in the letter he wrote to Pusey on the same day:

> I have just stopped by my own act R. Williams' translation of the Breviary, which he was recommencing in the Press, – but which he would not, unless I said I consented and that I could not do. But then the question comes, what will men do, if we let them do nothing?[9]

This suggests that Newman agreed with Keble that Williams was being 'overhasty' and that the time was not ripe for offering the Anglican Church a translation of the Roman Breviary. Robert Williams's own account was that he abandoned the translation because the project lacked Newman's agreement. This he explained to Bloxam in a letter of 20 July:

> I feel it impossible to proceed with the Breviary without Newman's full concurrence, and so others feel – Ward, Oakeley, and Wood. His judgement is worth all ours put together, and ought to be implicitly trusted. We may I think satisfy ourselves that it is well that it should be so. Anyhow it is a little check to a certain friend's ardour, which, let us hope may do him good.
>
> I therefore return the Letters of introduction, which I shall now have no occasion for, with many thanks to their writers. I had rather Mr. Ambrose Phillipps did not know my name . . . As for the copies of the Psalter, they are not sold. There are faults in the arrangements, which make them useless, and if ever the work is proceeded with, they must be cancelled.[10]

It would seem, on the evidence of Liddon, that some copies of the Psalter and the Proprium de Tempore for most of Advent were in fact sold. It is also clear that while the printed version of the translation finishes on page 192 (in the middle of a lesson of Matins for the 4th sunday of Advent), more of the translation had been completed in draft.[11] Robert Williams sent copies of the printed translation to Bloxam on 3 August 1841:

> I send you herewith 4 copies of the Breviary, so far as we have it finished. I send you more than one thinking you may like to show

> them to others, but I need not caution you to be careful to whom they are given. My first pages are not a good specimen. They contain little more than Psalms, and by no means give any idea of the real office as daily recited, as you are doubtless aware.
>
> The number of the saints has been so multiplied that the year is too short to commemorate them, so that the ancient arrangement of the psalter is practically superseded by the daily recurrence of Festivals. The Advent offices however are good specimens of the Part called the Proprium de Tempore. I wish you pleasure and profit in the use of these sheets . . .[12]

That Newman's intervention was decisive and his judgment implicitly trusted is borne out by his own brief reference to the ending of the project in the *Apologia*:

> At a comparatively early date I drew up the Tract on the Roman Breviary. It frightened my own friends on its first appearance; and several years afterwards, when younger men began to translate for publication the four volumes *in extenso*, they were dissuaded from doing so by advice to which from a sense of duty they listened.[13]

It is clear that it was for prudential reasons that Newman advised that the printing should not be resumed, for in the next sentence Newman praises the Breviary as 'that most wonderful and most attractive monument of the devotion of the saints.'

In 1842 Newman retired to Littlemore, probably regarding the project as finally at an end. Here, ironically, he and his companions began in April the daily recitation of the Roman Breviary, with certain omissions.

However, there was to be a third attempt to publish the proposed translation. This time the initiative came from Pusey, who was more convinced that one version of the Breviary should be translated for Anglicans. He had written to Newman after hearing of the latter's decision to stop the printing in 1841:

> I was in hopes that Rb. Wms. was at work at a Paris breviary in a form consistent with our formularies since the Reformation (Ed. VI 1st book).[14]

Pusey's initiative began in 1843. He was not unwilling to take the lead in this matter now that Newman had retired from the project. Pusey had been greatly affected by the loss of his daughter Catherine in 1833 and of his wife in 1839, and had withdrawn as much as possible from public life to devote himself to prayer and scholarship. He busied himself with translating Roman Catholic devotional works adapted for the use of the English Church, feeling convinced that Anglicans were in need of such spiritual nourishment. This was not without precedent among Anglican divines in the past, some of whom like Andrewes and Sherlock were aware of the spiritual riches of ancient liturgies, including the Missal and the Breviary.[15]

As part of this programme, Pusey considered publishing a translation of the Roman Breviary, and he made enquiries of Oakeley regarding the progress made in the earlier attempts. Oakeley replied on 20 November 1843, saying that the translation had been abandoned three years ago (actually in July 1841) 'at Newman's, or rather Mr. Keble's desire', that the whole translation was in manuscript except the hymns, which he (Oakeley) had undertaken to translate. 'Nothing retards the work but want of money.'[16]

Evidently Oakeley was prepared to take on the translation of the hymns which Newman had not translated. Isaac Williams, who had translated hymns from the Parisian Breviary, was also asked by Pusey to provide translations. Pusey wrote to him in December 1843:

> Perhaps you have heard that I have been revising our old plan, and J. K., Copeland and I have been in negotiation with Oakeley and R. Williams about a Breviary. Everything is going on very promisingly and I hope something will come of it soon; but it is better not talked about lest it be hindered. It is of course to be adapted to our Church.[17]

Pusey continued to consult Isaac Williams about details of the project, such as prayers for the dead, the calendar, the feasts of saints, and the feasts of the Blessed Virgin. On the whole, Isaac Williams was encouraging on these matters. He assured Pusey that he was already engaged in translating some of the hymns. 'All the rest Copeland has undertaken, but knowing how diffident and uncertain he is, I must see and secure you an answer from him.[18]

Though not in favour of the project, Newman seemed willing to allow his translations to be used. Samuel Wood, who had died in 1843, had bequeathed the manuscripts of his translation to Robert Williams. The latter was prepared to allow Pusey the use of his own manuscripts and those of Samuel Wood, although he was apparently not in favour of the revived project. Presumably Williams still felt bound by Newman's judgment of 1841. It was also the case that he was then moving away from his High Church convictions towards a Low Church stance. To the annoyance of Pusey and Oakeley, he vacillated considerably and awkwardly before making up his mind to allow the use of the manuscripts. William Copeland, in charge of the Littlemore church after Newman's resignation from St Mary's, had been enlisted to work with Pusey and Oakeley on the translation. All this can be inferred from a letter from Pusey to Copeland written from Ilfracombe on 5 July 1844:

> You will be glad to hear that R.W. will make any use of our friend Wood's MSS of the Breviary we wish, trusting to us that we must know what is wanted for our Church more than he. So then, as soon as the Hymns of the Passion are done, I hope you will set to work about this, and first of all see if you think there is anything, here and there, in N.'s hymns which he would like to retract, and then we could begin printing at once. I am anxious not to lose time . . .[19]

It is not clear how Pusey intended to finance the publication of the translation, whether he had engaged a printer or approached a publisher. Perhaps he intended to use his own financial resources.

Before encouraging Copeland and Oakeley to begin work on the translation, Pusey consulted both Newman and Keble. To Newman he wrote concerning his proposal to dedicate his edition of Avrillon's *Guide for Passing Lent Holily* to the Church of England. He also brought up the question of the translation project. Newman replied on the same date, 2 December 1843. He advised against it for the sake of the Church of England, but did not attempt to prevent it or persuade Pusey to abandon the project. It is a candid letter and shows how his thinking had developed:

> Your proposed Dedication has put it into my head to say to you what it did not strike me before to do – though I certainly think I ought.
>
> It is this. I am quite of opinion that any Breviary, however corrected, etc., will tend to prepare minds for the Church of Rome. I fully think that you will be doing so by your publication. Considering the strong feeling you are going to express, I ought not to fail to state this impression of mine. I do not think our system will bear it. It is like sewing a new piece of cloth on an old garment. Did I wish to promote the cause of the Church of Rome I should say, Do what you propose to do.
>
> I have before now been of another opinion. If it seems wonderful to you that I should change right round without showing distress at the intention expressed from time to time of editing Breviaries, I feel I must account for it in a way which will pain you – that my dislike of approximating Rome has diminished with my hope of avoiding her. Now, as before, *I* am not unwilling that Breviaries should be published – though for different reasons; but, as I have tried, while I had a charge in our Church, to do nothing against her, so now . . . you should hear my opinion on the subject.[20]

Liddon's comment on the different viewpoints of the two men is very pertinent:

> Of course, Newman's letter did not convince Pusey. Newman meant that Rome was alone the true home of all that Pusey wished to secure for the English Church by his adapted books. Pusey, believing that the English Church was Catholic, believed she had a right to and could assimilate all that was really Catholic in the devotional literature of the Church of Rome. It would raise the tone of the whole English Church; it would not make individuals disloyal to her. It would influence the devotional life of the English Church, as the publication of the 'Library of the Fathers' was influencing her theology. Newman, of course, could not agree.[21]

The following undated letter appears to be Pusey's reply to Newman. After discussing the dedication, he wrote:

With regard to the Breviary, K. gives up all idea, apparently, of attempting to translate words containing the mention of intercession, merits, perfection. So then the only addition to the character of the devotions would be 1) prayers for the departed, 2) a distinct office with relation to the Holy Eucharist, 3) bringing out more into life the Communion of Saints by their days and signs, 4) the praise of S. Mary. Of this last, with a people uninstructed on it, I have misgivings, and have been led to doubt, whether for the present, it wd. not be better to omit all the black letter days. The services for the great festivals and Lent, would alone be of great value; ... But then, you note in your sermons speaking of Patristic theology without some strong safeguard, leading towards Rome. If then I am only instrumental in procuring so much of the Breviary for our Church as is on the Patristic line, I am not doing more than we have all been doing for years ... [next section crossed out by Pusey:]

But then I should like to ask you

1) whether you think it wrong in accordance with my feelings to have any hand in giving any portion of the Breviary to our Church. I do not know how far Oakeley or Copeland might be influenced by my wishes; K. I shd think was not. You will be interested to see his ideas of what might be done wh. I inclose.

2) ... 3) ...

But now, my very dear N, I cannot bear to write what may perplex or pain you, or draw out things painful to say. You have pain enough all around you to make one's heart ache. I have been so accustomed to lean on you, that, in any difficulty, I involuntarily turn to you. I had rather go on, as best I can, by myself than say things to aggravate your pain. I half dread opening a note for fear I should have given you pain somehow. So, I pray you, by all the mercies God had shown me thro' these 20 years, do not let me add to all your distress. I send you this after all that you may see my mind, but never mind my questions. God turn all this heavy night into day.[22]

On 18 December 1843 Newman wrote to Pusey from Littlemore:

I have been intending to answer your most kind and affectionate note ever since it came, and now I am driven up into a corner for time. I must seem very cold and reserved to you – the truth is I have not had courage to tell you all I think. This has lasted a very long time – for years. Indeed, one has no right to scatter about one's own

> notions, when they are recent, lest they should be accidental and random. But some time or other I must tell you. And perhaps I must choose some serious season, as I do for telling you as much as this.
>
> Whether the publication of a Breviary is to lead our Church towards Rome or individuals in it (which is your question) can only be decided by experiment. It is like attempting to bend a stick; if it does not bend, it will break. If you do not move the whole Church, to a certainty you are moving individuals: there is no medium. Now in calculating the prospective resistance, the fact that the Bishops are adverse to the Breviary, and that some have pledged themselves against it, is a very anxious fact. Again, you must take into account generally the opposition of the nation to Rome. I do not think it enough, according to *my* feeling of the matter, to say, 'I leave it to a higher power whether or not He leads our Church to Rome, in consequence of my act'; I think you must contemplate another alternative and say, 'I think it right, and therefore leave it to Him altogether and absolutely what becomes of my act, whether He overrule it to the movement of the whole Church or of individuals in it, more or fewer.' I am only stating *my* feeling.
>
> Things have so silently changed (e.g. the fact of the Bishops' Charges, the secret growth of Roman tendencies in various minds, &c.) that I had not very fully mastered my own thoughts about the publication of a Breviary now, till your proposed Dedication made me realize them.
>
> . . . As to the Fathers . . . I *do* now think, far more than I did, that their study leads to Rome. It has thus wrought in me . . .[23]

Pusey had a considerable correspondence on this with John Keble, who was more encouraging – surprisingly so considering the part he is supposed to have played in the termination of the project in July 1841. He now seemed less worried about the possibility of offending Anglican feelings or of exerting a Romeward influence. However, he sent Pusey a long letter listing the omissions which would have to be made to make the Breviary acceptable to Anglicans. At the same time he was against altering anything which was retained.[24] It seems that Newman's letters had caused Pusey some disquiet about whether the publication would conflict with the position of the Church of England. On 9 January 1844 Keble wrote to Pusey:

With regard to the risk of publishing an English Breviary at all, even in the most expurgated shape, I own I cannot well comprehend it: that is, I cannot comprehend how it should have a Romeward tendency with good sort of persons: but to say that our Church cannot bear such a book, and that it is inconsistent with loyalty to her, this, it seems to me, *would* be a very scandalizing sort of thing. As to the services of St. Mary in particular, I can better comprehend your difficulty: even as an 'oikonomia' to reconcile people to the Breviary generally, it seems that it might be desirable to omit *them*: but why should this extend to *all* the black-letter-days? unless it be that you would not like to exclude (so far) the greatest Saint whilst you are honouring the rest? and I do not know that I could answer this very well. Yet it does seem to me that leaving out such a body of holy commemorations will *enormously* diminish the beauty and utility of the book. But still I would have it go on, and as you say, if the plan be a truly good one, more Saints' days may perhaps be added hereafter. Any hymns or other passages which you wish, I will of course try to translate; but they must be sent to me in good time, as I am very slow in such works, and getting more and more so.[25]

He wrote again on 15 January:

. . . The great question with me in these matters is, What has the Church really ordered and sanctioned? If I were satisfied that the Church Catholic really decreed all that the Breviary (e.g.) says of St. Mary, I fancy I see how a 'commoda interpretatio' might be made of it, consistent with other truths and duties. As it is, I shrink back, and dare not reason much on the point, nor take the devotional words which imply it in my mouth. My wish is, especially in my state of ignorance, to keep up a kind of neutrality as to the points in which we differ from Rome, and I very much wished the *British Critic* might have been kept up on that principle: by adhering to which and trying to live as holily as possible, I suppose an ordinary person may hope to be guided aright in our present most unhappy state.[26]

John Keble discussed these matters with Tom and probably others. In a letter to Tom dated 23 January 1844 he asked:

Also, do you think there is reason in objecting *generally* to the publication of RC books of devotion and devotional morality, however purified, from what our Church disapproves or seems to disapprove? e.g. Quesnal, as by Wilson; or a Reformed Breviary.

> Because Manning has been laying before Pusey objections by wholesale to *all* such things. What say you?[27]

Keble evidently had not lost all his reservations about the likely consequences and implications of the proposed translation, but on 22 February he wrote more encouragingly and even quoted his brother and sister in support of an edited Breviary, which is surprising in view of their previous firm opposition to the translation:

> In consequence of your report of Manning's view, I have asked two or three of those whom I suppose to be most dutiful to our Church, what they should think, in the abstract, of a reformed breviary – my sister and brother, for instance, and Judge Coleridge; and their answers are encouraging . . . On the whole, I feel as if it were more dutiful to our Church to go on. Really it would be quite scandalous for a *reformed* Breviary to be supposed inconsistent with her tone.[28]

The correspondence between Newman, Pusey and Keble reflects some misunderstandings and also considerable shifts of opinion by some of the leading figures. John Keble was now more supportive of the project generally, and his brother and sister less hostile to a modified version. Pusey was beginning to have conscientious doubts about the propriety of publishing the translation. Robert Williams was behaving awkwardly, it would seem, and Newman admitted for the first time that he no longer had any personal difficulty in accepting the whole of the Breviary, although doubtless his previous advice to Pusey against publishing on prudential grounds still held. However, in a letter to Pusey, written during March 1844 he offered to help:

> If it suits you, I would undertake the Breviary Hymns down to Dominica Passionis *exclusive* – i.e. (in addition to those printed) Christmas, Innocents, Epiphany, Lent, I suppose.[29]

Keble had referred in a letter to Pusey being 'pained' but had not made it clear to Newman what caused this. Newman wrote to Keble from Littlemore on 2 March 1844:

> If you allude to R.Williams and his Breviary plan as paining Pusey, I really know very little about it. I believe he is content to wait *any time*, but does not like to publish it with alterations or what he would call mutilations – and that from reverence for the Breviary. Perhaps I ought to add, though it will pain you, that for myself I have no difficulty in the Breviary *in toto*, though you are the first person to whom I say so.[30]

Keble replied to Newman the following day saying that he had not intended to refer to Williams and the Breviary project as causing pain to Pusey, but as a matter of fact Pusey was being troubled by Williams. At first Williams had seemed willing to work at the translation under Pusey's leadership. Then he had drawn back and would do no more than make Wood's and his own manuscripts available.

> Pusey is certainly *perplexed* by what R.Williams has lately written about the Breviary, because it seems to him and to me also not quite to agree with what he wrote to me before; but I think his, R.W.'s, feeling very natural and would not on any account press him against it. Pray tell P. this, if the subject is started between you, for I have just been writing to him and have not sufficiently expressed this. Of course Williams' drawing back is about as great a check to us as we could have, but it would be exceedingly painful, had he given way and repented afterwards. I don't think P. in what he wrote to me was thinking either of him or of Oakeley's St. Bernard, but rather of a plan which he hears Mr. Christie (Albany) has of publishing *Paradisus Animae* entire (I conclude in English) as also the *Horae Diurnae* . . .
>
> I should have been pained, I dare say, at what you say of your feelings about the Breviary, had I not supposed from former letters that you had laid aside your objections. My grand swallow of pain on the subject was perhaps three quarters of a year ago, when I received a long letter of yours and retired into a deserted old chalk pit to read it. I cannot tell you with what sort of fancy I look at the place now.[31]

The 'swallow of pain' referred to the letter written by Newman on 4 May 1843. There was a covering note beginning 'prepare for a shock . . .' In the letter, Newman wrote that after studying the Donatist history:

> It broke upon me that we were in a state of schism ... At present, I fear, as far as I can realize my own convictions, I consider the Roman Catholic communion the Church of the Apostles ... I am far *more* sure that England is in schism than that the Roman additions to the Primitive Creed may not be developments, arising out of a keen and vivid realizing of the Divine Depositum of faith.[32]

Probably Keble was not surprised to hear that Newman was able to accept the Breviary *in toto*. With Newman's withdrawal from the Church of England and his submission to the Roman Catholic Church in 1845, Pusey's hopes of publishing the Breviary translation were finally dashed. All there was to show for the labours of Newman, Wood, Williams and Oakeley were the sections of the translation which had been printed. Some of these were sewn into little booklets and bound in brown paper covers. According to Liddon they were sold in Oxford bookshops.[33]

The booklet is about 3½ inches x 5 inches, clearly and attractively printed, and well laid out. There is no title page. The contents begin with the Psalter arranged for the seven days of the week. This is followed by the Proper of the Season of Advent up to the Fourth Sunday, page 192, finishing in the middle of the sixth lesson of Matins. It was presumably printed by Messrs Lacy, Norton & Co.[34] The Hail Mary is given at the beginning. Nothing is omitted from Compline: the Marian antiphons are given in full, in a translation evidently that of Wood or Williams. The lessons not taken from the Bible, the rubrics, the collects, the antiphons and the versicles are also to be presumed to be the translations made by Wood or Williams. The hymns are given in Newman's translations, and the scriptural passages are taken from the Authorised Version. There are footnotes giving biblical references in the lessons and elsewhere.[35] It can only be a matter of regret that the translation was never completed. To judge from the section which was printed it would have been an excellent and attractive production. As it happened, numerous Anglican translations from the Breviary were produced during the nineteenth century.[36]

CHAPTER SIX

The Sarum Breviary Project

In addition to the project for translating the Roman Breviary, there was another project, associated mainly with Pusey, for publishing an edition of the Sarum Breviary in the Latin and also in English. Whether or not he was the original proponent of the scheme, Pusey emerged as the prime mover of it. He himself possessed a copy of the Sarum Breviary and was accustomed (probably from the time of his wife's final illness) to recite the little hours and Compline from it whenever he had time to do so as a supplement to the Prayer Book offices. According to Liddon,[1] he did not at first commend this practice to others lest it should promote dissatisfaction with the Prayer Book on account of its limited provision for the liturgical offices. But he came to support the proposal to publish, probably because of the liturgical riches he considered it to possess, and probably also because of the growing interest in the origins of the Book of Common Prayer. This interest was particularly stimulated by Lloyd's lectures and Palmer's *Origines Liturgicae*.

The Sarum project was first mooted in 1839 and 1840. It was seen by some, such as Bowden, as something of a compromise following the failure of the first attempt to publish a translation of the Roman Breviary. The Sarum Breviary was considered to be more acceptable to Anglicans than the Roman Breviary. It could be considered to be part of the Anglican heritage, at least by Anglicans willing to look beyond Cranmer for the origins of the Prayer Book. Cranmer had based his daily offices on the Use of Sarum, making many adaptations, but also retaining some interesting features from that Use. Among Anglicans, the Sarum Breviary had officially fallen out of use when superseded by the

Prayer Book. Among Roman Catholics it fell out of use as English priests, whether abroad or on the English mission, came to use other breviaries, especially the Breviarium Romanum issued by Pius V in 1568. Because of the conditions in sixteenth-century England, no attempt was made by Roman Catholics to secure the continued use of the Sarum Breviary under the provisions of the Bull *Quod a nobis* (1568) which allowed for missals and breviaries with at least two hundred years of continuous use to continue to be used.

The Sarum Breviary had not been reprinted since the sixteenth century and copies were difficult to find. Many breviaries must have been destroyed in 1549 when the old service books were ordered to be burnt. There was therefore good reason to publish a new edition for study at least, if not for devotional use. It had not been 'reformed' in accordance with the decrees of Pius V, and could be regarded as medieval and not 'Romish'. Being prior to both the Reformation and the Counter-Reformation, it was a less controversial book. It was of English provenance, although in fact it was a variant of the medieval Roman office.

Nineteenth-century scholars would have noticed the similarities and the differences between the Sarum Breviary and the modern Roman Breviary. The general structure and the psalter were the same, and the bulk of the Proper and the lectionary was common to both.[2] There were considerable differences in the Calendar, particularly in the Sanctoral. Sarum had more variety at Compline. It was also noteworthy for its hymnary. There was much variety in the hymnaries used throughout Europe in the Middle Ages. The Sarum hymnary contained 119 hymns: in general, the selection of hymns was well made, and represented the best hymns in the older English hymnaries and in the universal church. It was a restrained collection, lacking the extravagant and decadent hymns which were to be found in some of the Continental medieval breviaries. The Sarum hymns were in the original Latin version, not in the 'corrected' version imposed upon the Roman Breviary by Urban VIII in 1629. Urban's hymnary contained 98 hymns; by 1972 when the

Roman Breviary was suppressed, the number of hymns had increased to about 171. The Roman Breviary in the 1830s therefore contained more hymns than the Sarum, and these were a mixture of ancient hymns as 'corrected' by Urban VIII and modern office hymns which varied greatly in character and worth. Generally the Sarum hymnary was preferable, and would have had a considerable appeal to Pusey and his friends at Oxford with a classical education.

In many ways this was an attractive project, but it was also the case that the Sarum Breviary was as much in need of reform as other medieval breviaries had been. The Pian reform of 1568 was unfortunately rather limited in scope and conservative in character, but it did introduce certain much-needed improvements from which the Sarum Breviary would have benefited. Cranmer had in fact drawn up two schemes for reforming the Sarum office.[3] However, Pusey and his friends would only have wanted to 'reform' the Sarum Breviary by the omission of elements unacceptable to Anglican belief.

On 21 February 1840, Pusey wrote to John Keble:

> I have undertaken to ask your opinion about the following plans.
> (a) Publishing the Salisbury Breviary in the original as a document, and as less likely to invite people to Rome than the Roman, which is said to be now in much use.
> (b) Publishing the S.B., but marking what cannot be shown to be Catholic, either by inclosing it in brackets or by omitting it in the text and putting it in a note at the foot of the page.
> (c) *Translating* the S.B., reformed upon certain principles, as admitting nothing which is controversial, except what has the sanction of Edward the Sixth's first book. This would admit of the Prayers for the Departed Saints, and the mention of the name of the Blessed Virgin in commemoration, but exclude the mention of the intercession of the Saints.
> (d) Publishing the S.B. (original), either entire, or as in (b), at the same time with (c). It was thought that it might be understood that only (c) was recommended for use; (a) or (b) was published as a document only. (The plan is that of the younger men.)[4]

Keble's reply is not extant, but he presumably gave the proposal qualified support, for Newman commented favourably on the plan in a letter of 17 March 1840 to Pusey:

> I am very pleased at your and K's plan about the Salisbury Breviary. It is important that we should be beforehand with the R.C.'s in doing it. I have a repugnance to mutilating or garbling it, considering we abuse the SPCK for doing so towards Bishop Wilson. The plan of first giving the text, and then adjusting it to K. Edward's first book, seems to get over the difficulty without seeming to recommend what we do not wish.[5]

The choice of the 1549 Prayer Book as the criterion of 'adjustment' would have been regarded by some critics as arbitrary and controversial, as it was the least 'reformed' of the Prayer Books. It was chosen by Keble and Pusey to give themselves as much scope as possible for being Catholic within the Church of England. The Tractarians often showed a marked preference for this first Prayer Book for the same reason.[6]

It would seem that Keble's reservations about the Sarum Breviary increased. By the end of March he supported the publication of the whole of the Latin version as a document, but the translation to consist of only a selection of parts for devotional use, with nothing controversial being included. He wrote to Pusey on 30 March:

> I have been into Winchester today, and spent some time in endeavouring to find out a Sarum Breviary which professes to be in the College Library; but as that is in great disorder at present I could not light upon it. I do not like putting off my answer to your last note any longer; and therefore I think I am ready to say that I should approve of the publication of it as a document, and of a selection of parts to be translated for a devotional book, on the principle of taking such things only as are virtually sanctioned by Edward the Sixth's first book. It seems to me that in this way we go as nearly as we can expect to providing our readers with the good of the Breviary without the harm of the more irreverent parts.[7]

This was obviously more rigorously selective than Pusey had in mind. It was considered a discouraging response and Pusey also came to have his own reservations, as he told Newman:

> For myself, I do not object to the plan; but should hardly like to be prominent. I have fears for our people, until I hear more of their acting up to the principles of our Church, fasting, &c.[8]

It was proposed to publish the translation by subscription, but the plan fell through.

There was evidently a revival of the plan to publish the Latin text of the Sarum Breviary, for in a letter dated 4 June 1841 Robert Williams asked Bloxam to remind Oakeley 'to bring up the copy of the Sarum Breviary, from which Seager is going to reprint for me'.[9] Charles Seager, a learned Orientalist 'steeped in recondite knowledge of all kinds',[10] spent four years as Pusey's assistant Hebrew lecturer before joining the Roman Catholic Church in October 1843. Seager's edition of the Sarum Breviary was never completed. Only two sections appeared. In 1842 the Fasciculus Primus was published, containing the Psalterium and the Ordinarium; the Vigiliae Mortuorum; and the Proprium de Tempore for Advent. In the preface, he thanked those who had supplied money for the publication. After that he seemed to have delayed doing any further work on it, perhaps feeling less interested now that he was a Catholic. He evidently consulted various friends about the possibility of continuing. Newman wrote in a letter to Ambrose St John from Maryvale 14 July 1848:

> Tell Seager with my kindest regards that you think I should be against his proceeding with the Salisbury Breviary – but don't tell him (for I am not bound to tell him, nor would a confessor tell him) that I *do* think he should make some satisfaction for the money he wasted – or at least draw up a statement of account for one's satisfaction.[11]

This was in reply to St John who had written on 6 July:

> Seager wishes me to tell you that chiefly acting on what you said in Paris,he thinks it his duty to publish as much as he can of the Salisbury Breviary at his own cost, he seems inclined to do this partly because any explanation sent to former subscribers would he feels set them all talking and make matters worse, and secondly

> because it will be a document when done which will be useful for posterity. I think from his tone he is acting under direction in doing this, but is seems a great pity, and waste of time.[12]

Eventually Seager published the Fasciculus Secundus, containing the Commune Sanctorum and Officia B.V.M., in 1855.[13] From the Primus Fasciculus, Procter took the office for the First Sunday in Advent in his *History of the Book of Common Prayer*.[14]

The first complete edition of the Latin text to be published since the reign of Mary was that of Procter and Wordsworth.[15] This was based on the Chevallon edition of 1531, the last edition of the Great Breviary, of which six copies were known to have escaped the destruction of service books in 1549.

The proposals made by Pusey and Williams for a translation of the whole, or of selected parts of, the Sarum Breviary came to nothing. With the growth of religious communities in the Church of England during the nineteeth century, various office books were produced, many of them drawing on the text of Sarum to a greater or lesser degree.[16] The first and only complete translation of the Sarum Breviary was made by Sister Amelia Warren of the Society of the Most Holy Trinity who worked on it from 1854 until just before her death in 1869. This Society was established in 1848, with Pusey as its spiritual guide and loyal supporter. The translation was not published until 1889 and was not sold to the general public.[17] For the hymns, use was made of translations by Newman, Caswall, Copeland and Chambers.

CHAPTER SEVEN

The Breviary Offices at Littlemore

Since accepting the living of St Mary's in 1828, Newman had regularly walked or ridden to Littlemore to take services, give talks and visit his parishioners. Against opposition he eventually succeeded in opening a daughter church in the village in 1836. The first time he actually resided in the village was in 1840 when he spent Lent there, living in lodgings with the Barnes family. He devoted himself to prayer and fasting, and recited privately the full Breviary offices. Presumably by now he was familiar with the use of the Breviary and the structure of the daily office, and had become accustomed to praying at length in Latin. One cannot imagine Newman rushing through the prayers, and the recitation of the Hours must have taken a considerable part of his day.[1]

In 1841 also he spent Lent at Littlemore, but had to return frequently to Oxford. In 1842 he again spent Lent at Littlemore. He practised great austerities but to his regret was unable to recite all the offices.

He also spent the summer of 1841 at Littlemore in the house known as St George's. About this time he bought the L-shaped block of stables which were to become his retreat. To his bishop he described it as a parsonage; popularly it became known as The College. The refurbishing was not completed until the spring of 1842. Newman spent Lent 1842 in lodgings in Littlemore, moving into the College after Easter, on 19 April. He was on his own for the first two days, but then other occupants arrived; John Dobrée Dalgairns, William Lockhart, and Frederick Bowles in 1842; later Ambrose St John and

Charles Brooke Bridges came, and towards the end Richard Stanton, Albany Christie and John Walker. Thomas Meyrick stayed only one day because of illness. All of these men later became Roman Catholics and all except Bridges became priests. Others came and stayed for various periods as guests, and many more came as visitors.

Newman intended the house at Littlemore to be a simple residence where young men who shared his views, especially if they were being denied fellowships or holy orders or, as in the case of Dalgairns, the support of their families because of their association with the Oxford Movement, could retire to pray, study, reflect, and practise mortification. The recitation of the Breviary in common was an outstanding feature of each day, and made a great impression on each of those who wrote their reminiscences of life at Littlemore. Newman derived his belief in a life of prayer, fasting and mortification not from contemporary monasticism, about which he knew very little, but from the spirit of the primitive Church. He also hoped to hold back over-enthusiastic young men from going over to Rome by providing them with an environment away from Oxford where they could reflect on their position as Anglicans. Newman deprecated any idea of the house being a monastery. It was simply a residence where the community lived quietly, prayerfully, and moderately austerely. There were few rules and little supervision. The life of the little community rested on a spirit of co-operation and voluntary participation in the various activities – the offices, meditation, fasting, study, and so on. An important element in the life at Littlemore was reading, especially the study of the Fathers, and it was for this purpose that Newman built up his remarkable library, which always seemed to be overflowing and requiring more room.

The earliest accounts of life at Littlemore were given in letters to a friend by the first young man to join Newman, the enthusiastic John Dobrée Dalgairns.[2] He described clearly the ethos and objectives of the house, and demolished the myth of the 'pseudo-monastery'. Newman also had to counter the same rumour when he reassured Bishop Bagot of Oxford that he had not established an 'Anglo-Catholic monastery'. He explained that he had simply built a 'parsonage house' in which he planned to live quietly for a while. There were at least as many parishioners in Littlemore as at St Mary's, he told the bishop, and added:

> With a view to personal improvement, I was led more seriously to a design which has long been on my mind. For many years, at least thirteen, I have wished to give myself a life of greater regularity than I have hitherto led . . . At the same time of course it would be a great comfort to me to know that God has put it into the hearts of others to pursue their personal edification in the same way, and unnatural not to wish to have the benefit of their presence and encouragement.[3]

Bagot readily accepted Newman's explanations, but rumours were rife that, as Newman put it in the *Apologia*,

> I was actually in the service of the enemy. I had been already received into the Catholic Church, and was rearing at Littlemore a nest of Papists, who, like me, were to take the Anglican oaths which they did not believe, and for which they got dispensation from Rome, and thus in due time were to bring over to that unprincipled Church great numbers of the Anglican clergy and laity. Bishops gave their countenance to this imputation against me. The case was simply this: as I made Littlemore a place of retirement for myself, so did I offer it to others. There were young men in Oxford whose testimonials for Orders had been refused by their colleges; there were young clergymen who had found themselves unable from conscience to go on with their duties, and had thrown up their pastoral engagements. Such men were already going straight to Rome, and I interposed; . . . I interposed from fidelity to my clerical engagements, and from duty to my bishop; and from the interest which I was bound to take in them, and from belief that they were premature or excited. Their friends besought me to quiet them, if I could. Some of them came to live with me at Littlemore. They were laymen, or in the place of laymen. I kept some of them back for several years from being received into the Catholic Church. Even when I had given up my living, I was still bound by my duty to their parents or friends, and I did not forget still to do what I could for them. The immediate cause of my resigning St. Mary's was the unexpected conversion of one of them. After that, I felt it was

> impossible to keep my post there, for I had been unable to keep my word with my bishop.[4]

The atmosphere of this austere house was carefully tended by Newman and was the opposite of the caricatures circulated by his detractors. There was to be peace, calm, reflection and prayer. These young men were able to withdraw from a world of controversy and misunderstanding, of criticism, attack and uncertainty, to a quiet and simple community life where they experienced respect, sympathy and consideration. Newman failed entirely to hold any of them back from Rome; but the help they received from the life at Littlemore is amply testified in their letters and memoirs. Newman himself was to write of Littlemore:

> I have been most happy there, though in a state of suspense. And there it has been that I have both been taught my way and received an answer to my prayers.[5]

Prayer was an essential element in the ethos of the Littlemore community. Newman chose to make the offices of the Roman Breviary the basis of this life of prayer. It might have been thought that this was an unsuitable choice in view of Newman's earlier worries about the Romanising tendencies of the Breviary and his desire to hold men back from Rome. His decision was doubtless due to his great admiration for the Breviary as an incomparable source of rich and extensive liturgical prayer. The use of the offices at Littlemore must be understood in this context: Newman's emphasis on a life of prayer and his belief in the value of the daily offices of the Roman Breviary. His companions were, in some cases, already familiar with the Breviary and doubtless enthusiastic to recite it in common – something they would have had very little opportunity to do hitherto.

The community attended the parish church in Littlemore for Holy Communion and the Prayer Book offices of Morning and Evening Prayer. The Breviary offices and the meditation took place in the 'oratory', the room next to Newman's. It was about 12 feet square, with the windows boarded up for privacy and the walls hung with red damask. At one end there was a quasi-altar – a ledge with a Spanish crucifix and a pair of candlesticks. This 'altarino' had an ante-pendium of white challis. Along the centre of the room was a board on which the community would rest their office books. The oratory was lit by candles in a tall branch-candlestick.

The daily horarium varied from time to time. Lockhart put on record the practice of the earlier period at Littlemore:

> I was admitted, by Newman's great kindness, as one of his first companions at Littlemore. I remained with him about a year. The life was something like what we had read of in the *Lives of the Fathers of the Desert* – of prayer, fasting, and study. We rose at midnight to recite the Nocturnal office of the Roman Breviary. I remember, direct invocation of Saints was omitted, and instead we asked God that the Saint of the day might pray for us. I think we passed an hour in private prayer, and, for the first time, I learned what *meditation* meant. We fasted every day till twelve, and in Lent and Advent till five. There was some mitigation on Sundays and the greater festivals. We went to Communion at the village church and to the service there, morning and evening, every day; we went to Confession every week.[6]

The prayerful atmosphere at Littlemore was described vividly by Frederick Oakeley:

> It was my own privilege to pass more than once a week or so with Dr. Newman in that retreat; and who that remembers the feeling of religious composure which pervaded it; the library with its look, nay its very smell, of theological work; its studious inmates, each at his own table with his folio; its silence made audible by the ticking of the clock on the chimney-piece; – or who, again, that has ever partaken of the frugal meal (still in silence) in the unfurnished refectory, or assisted at the Hours in the dark little chapel, with its high red curtain, its crucifix, and its air of impenetrable seclusion – but must acknowledge that here at any rate there was no 'sham'? Surely it was the ascetism of the Desert leading up to Christ![7]

In the 1880s the indefatigable chronicler Bloxam wrote to as many old friends as possible asking them to write out all they could remember of Littlemore. The replies of Lockhart, Stanton and Christie were copied into his notebooks, and it is remarkable that they made particular mention of the Breviary offices.[8]

In 1842 Newman jotted down a timetable which was perhaps a norm rather than a record since other records show variations in detail:

5 – 6½	Matins and Lauds
6½ – 7	Breakfast
7 – 7½	Prime
7½ – 10	Study, etc., with Tierce
10 – 11	Morning Prayers – Chapel
11 – 2	Study, etc., with Sext
2 – 3	Recreation
3 – 3¾	Evening Prayer – Chapel
3¾ – 4½	Recreation
4½ – 6	Study, etc., with None
6 – 6½	Supper
6½ – 7½	Recreation
7½ – 9½	Study, etc.
9½ – 10	Vespers
10 – 10¼	Compline
10¼ – 5	Sleep, etc.

No talking except between 2 and 7½.[9]

Mark Pattison also left a detailed account of the recitation of the offices at Littlemore. For some time in 1838–9 he lived with other young men in the house in St Aldates set up by Newman and Pusey. Here he met Seager, and it is likely that he was introduced to the Breviary by him. He became for a number of years a devoted follower of Newman and Pusey, and this included the recitation of the Breviary. He recorded this in his *Memoirs*, which reflect his later anti-Tractarian feeling:

> I adopted the plan which many others did of reciting the Hours of the Roman Breviary, and seemed to please myself for some time in this time-wasting and mind-drowning occupation.[10]

Pattison had already visited Littlemore at least once, on 8 January 1839, before spending a fortnight as a guest at the College in October 1843. Precise details about the offices were recorded in his diary:

> Saturday September 30th: Vespers at 8, Compline at 9.
> Sunday October 1st: St. John called me at 5.30, and at 6 went to Matins, which with Lauds and Prime took about an hour and a half ... Terce at 9, and at 11 to Church – Communion ... Vespers at 8, Compline at 9, the clocks here very backward.[11]

It is interesting that Pattison's entry for 6 October is entered as 'St. Faith in the Salisbury Breviary', although it is not known whether he possessed a copy of the Sarum Breviary, perhaps through the influence of Seager, or whether there was a copy at Littlemore. St Faith is given in the Calendar of the Book of Common Prayer.[12]

One of the later entrants, Richard Stanton, who arrived on 20 June 1845, recorded his experience of life at Littlemore towards the end, from which it seems that the observances had not changed much:

> The plan of life they followed was simple in the extreme ... There was no written rule, but everything went on in the same course day after day. Mr. Newman, who would allow no affectation of monastic titles, was still commonly called the vicar ... Perfect silence was observed in the house, except during the recreation in the library after dinner. The whole of the Breviary Office was said in the Oratory, though not according to the Roman Calendar, and with the omission, I think, of the Suffragia Sanctorum, and the final antiphon of Our Lady, as being expressly contrary to the Anglican Articles. Matins were said at an early hour in the morning; and I have been told that, during the Advent of 1842, they had made the experiment of rising at midnight for this purpose, on the persuasion of Dalgairns, who had an enthusiastic admiration of the Cistercian Rule.[13] Mr. Newman, however, considered that it would be imprudent to continue the practice, and it was abandoned. Besides this, we went twice a day to the Anglican service in the village church. The morning was devoted to study in the library ... Mr. Newman was known to be engaged on his work, which afterwards

> appeared as the *Essay on Development*, and usually devoted about fourteen hours a day to the task ... We took our breakfast standing in the dining-room, and some luncheon also in the middle of the day. In the afternoon it was usual to take a walk, and sometimes Mr. Newman accompanied us, and kept up a most delightful conversation ... Dinner was at five o'clock with reading, the book at this time being some work of Blosius. Then followed recreation ... in the library, and tea, a most refreshing break in the long silence of the day.[14]

It is possible, though not certain, that use was made of the translated section of the Breviary, bound in brown paper covers, which was all that had resulted from the Breviary translation project. Otherwise, the offices were recited in the Latin version, except that Compline was sometimes recited in English if visitors were present. The *Breviarium Romanum* was recited in full except for the Antiphons of the Blessed Virgin Mary and certain lesser omissions. The Latin was pronounced in the manner which they, as Oxford men, were accustomed to use. This was an Anglicised pronunciation in which the Latin vowels and consonants were mostly given the sounds of the corresponding English vowels and consonants. This was considered in keeping with their position as Anglicans. While they considered the Roman Breviary as much their heritage as that of Roman Catholics, they did not consider it necessary or fitting to adopt any 'Church Latin', or Italianate, pronunciation.[15]

The Breviary offices were recited continuously at Littlemore for some three years including the two years which Newman spent in lay communion after resigning the living of St Mary's and when he was working to complete his book *Essay on Development*. We can imagine that they greatly sustained Newman during this difficult period. These offices were still being recited by the residents when Father Dominic Barberi received Newman, Bowles and Stanton into the Roman Catholic Church on 9 October 1845. This was followed by a significant change in the office: the Antiphons of the Blessed Virgin Mary were now included, the various omissions at Prime restored, and the Italianate pronunciation of Latin adopted.[16] There is a graphic, though slightly inaccurate account, of this by Frederick Oakeley:

> It was a memorable day that of 9th October 1845. The rain came down in torrents . . . The wind, like a spent giant, howled forth the expiring notes of its equinoctial fury . . . The 'monastery' was more than usually sombre and still. Egress and ingress there were none that day; for it had been given out, among friends accustomed to visit there, that Mr. Newman 'wished to remain quiet'. One of these friends, who resided in the neighbourhood, had been used to attend the evening office in the oratory of the house, but he was forbidden to come 'for two or three days, for reasons which would be explained later'. The 9th of the month passed off without producing any satisfaction to the general curiosity. All that transpired was that a remarkable-looking man, evidently a foreigner, and shabbily dressed in black, had asked his way to Mr. Newman's on the day but one before; and the rumour was that he was a Catholic priest. In the course of a day or two the friend before mentioned was readmitted to the evening office, and found that a change had come over it. The Latin was pronounced for the first time in the Roman way, and the antiphons of Our Lady, which up to that day had always been omitted, came out in their proper place. The friend in question would have asked the reason of these changes, but it was forbidden to speak to any of the community after night-prayers. Very soon the mystery was cleared up by Mr. Newman and his companions appearing at mass in the public chapel at Oxford. He had been received into the Church on the 9th by Father Dominic, of the Congregation of the Passion. Thus noiselessly and unobtrusively did the event come to pass which . . . must be pronounced to have been, if not the providential end of the Tractarian Movement, at any rate the symbol and measure of its true significance.[17]

CHAPTER EIGHT

Newman's Writings on the Daily Office

This chapter is a review of Newman's works on the daily office. It begins with an account of Tract 75 on the Roman Breviary. This is followed by some notes on the hymns of the breviary and a discussion of Newman's Prefaces to the two volumes of *Hymni Ecclesiae*. His translations of Latin office hymns are dealt with next and finally there are some comments on his Parochial Sermon 'The Daily Service'.

Tract 75

Entitled 'On the Roman Breviary as embodying the substance of the devotional services of the Church Catholic', this Tract was first published on 24 June 1836 and addressed *ad clerum*. It consisted of 148 pages. In the second and subsequent editions it was enlarged to 207 pages. Newman atttributed the origins of this Tract to Hurrell Froude, but no manuscript by Froude has survived, and it seems clear that Newman composed the Tract having studied Froude's Breviary and having made notes from Gavanti and Zaccaria in the Bodleian on 2 May 1836.[1] Newman must have worked very assiduously at the Tract for it to have been published some seven weeks after he began making notes in the Bodleian; perhaps he had worked on the Analysis of the office and the translations before making these notes.

The Tract was surprisingly popular and quickly ran through several editions.[2] Although Newman claimed that he produced the Tract for Froude's sake, he was clearly very enthusiastic himself about the Roman Breviary. This enthusiasm had come to Newman rather later than to some of his associates: Hurrell Froude, Wilberforce and Pusey were interested in the Breviary at least as early as 1827. Newman's interest in the Breviary dated only from 12 March 1836 when he acquired Froude's breviary.[3] It seems that he could not have done any work related to the Tract before that date, which makes the completion of the Tract and its publication on 24 June of the same year a remarkable achievement.

Newman's Tract can be described as especially typical of what the Tractarians were trying to achieve. Their aim was to show that the Church of England was in an intermediate position between modern Romanism and modern Protestantism, and that it had inherited a tradition which was both patristic and apostolic. Hence Newman's insistence that Anglicans belonged to the Church Catholic and had every right, indeed a duty, to avail themselves of the liturgical heritage of the Western Church. At the same time he insisted that Anglicans must dissociate themselves from certain objectionable elements which were characteristic not of the Church Catholic but of modern Romanism. Newman changed his views on this within a few years. He came to realise that, for him at least, it was pointless to conceive of a Breviary reformed for Anglicans: the Breviary could be accepted only in its fullness and this meant accepting all that Rome stood for. This was at the root of the 'Romanising' influence of the Roman Breviary which Newman later came to realise and to experience sharply himself.[4] But in 1836 he was still holding confidently the mainstream Tractarian position, that the Church of England could regain its position in the Church Catholic without embracing Rome.

At that time the Roman Breviary was not well known or readily available to the majority of Anglican clergy,[5] to many of whom Tract 75 was something of a revelation. There was considerable prejudice against the Breviary. It was considered not only thoroughly 'Romish' but also complicated and long, requiring arduous initiation into its use. Because of its complexity and its being in Latin, it was virtually a clerical preserve. It was not well adapted to use by the people. Many must have thought of it in the words of Cranmer that 'many times there was more business to find out what should be read, than to read it when it was found out'. This was an exaggeration, but there was much truth in this. Until the simplification of the daily office after the Second Vatican Council, it was difficult to recite it without recourse to an *ordo*.

Undaunted by the complexity of the Breviary, Newman set out in this Tract to urge the Church of England to resume the use of the Breviary offices, which he claimed had 'so much of excellence and beauty' despite 'certain additions and novelties' which had been introduced into them comparatively recently by the Church of Rome. The daily office, he argued, belonged to the Church Catholic, and not exclusively to the Romanists who 'by retaining it in its ancient Latin form . . . have defrauded the Church of that benefit which, in the vernacular tongue, it might have afforded the people at large'.

Newman gave other reasons for 're-appropriating' (as he put it) the Breviary offices. The daily offices of Morning and Evening Prayer in the Book of Common Prayer were derived from the Breviary offices: this was not generally understood at that time, which is why Palmer's exposition of the origins of the Prayer Book caused so much interest. So Newman argued that an acquaintance with the Breviary would add to an understanding of the Prayer Book offices. He also considered that the Breviary offices constituted an admirable form of private devotion. In addition, the recitation of these offices would 'impress many persons with a truer sense of the excellence and profitableness' of the psalms 'than it is the fashion of the age to entertain'.

Finally, and most interestingly, he hoped that if it could be shown that the 'corruptions' which had accrued to the Breviary were of a late date, then this would provide further evidence for 'discriminating and separating off the Roman from the primitive Church'.

In advocating a return to the Breviary offices, Newman doubtless caused surprise to many of his contemporaries; and yet this was seen by him as part of the process by which the

Plate 3 Another photograph of Newman's room at the Birmingham Oratory, showing his hinged writing desk and, immediately in front, his collection of breviaries.

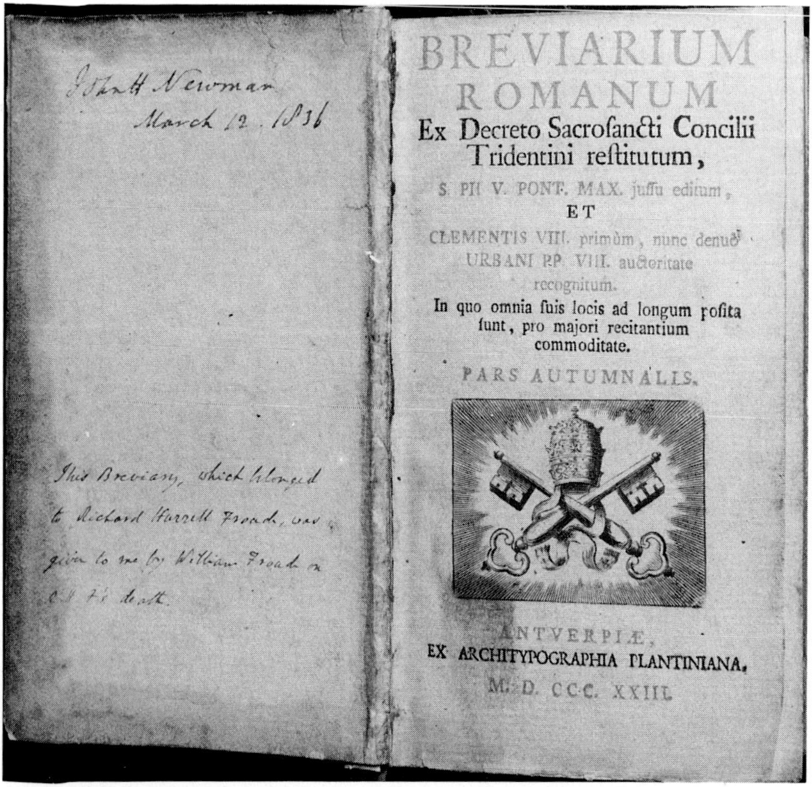

Plate 4 The title page of Volume 1 of Froude's breviary which Newman acquired in 1836. Note Newman's inscription, just visible on the opposite page.

Church of England was to regain its full catholicity and restore a liturgical structure to its worship. This part of the programme of the Oxford Movement was largely achieved, for by the end of the century various forms of the daily office were being used by the many Anglican religious orders which had developed, by many of the clergy, and by some of the laity.[6]

But in 1836 Newman was writing for clerics unfamiliar with the actual contents of the Breviary. Accordingly much of Tract 75 is taken up with a survey and descriptive analysis of the offices. To illustrate this, he gave selections from typical offices set out in detail in an English translation. He gave the complete office from Matins to Compline for Sunday, 21 June 1801, which in that year was the fourth Sunday after Pentecost. He followed this with a weekday office, in more summary form, namely the first Monday in Advent, and with parts of the office for 6 August (the Transfiguration) and 10 August (St Laurence). Then he gave two offices in English of his own designing: Matins for Bishop Ken's day (21 March) and an office of the dead. The latter was carefully styled 'Service in commemoration of the Dead in Christ', and to make it clear that he maintained the traditional Anglican objections to intercession for the dead he stated in a preamble

> that the complaints and supplications contained in the Psalms and Lessons selected are introduced in memory of those temporal miseries, especially in sickness and dying, from which death opens an escape.

Finally he gave the proper parts of the office for the Sundays and weekdays of Advent.

Newman praised the general excellence of the Breviary, but at the same time attacked strongly the features which he then considered to be objectionable. In particular he deprecated the intercessions of Mary and the Saints, and all hymns, antiphons and offices in honour of Mary. He condemned the excessive number of hagiographical lessons, especially those containing apocryphal or incredible material. He regretted that the

scriptural reading did not encompass the whole Bible in any one year. This was due to various factors, such as the accumulation of other readings, patristic and hagiographical, which impinged on the space allotted to biblical readings, and the tendency to shorten readings. Another factor was the multiplication of saints days on the Calendar, which meant that the cursus of the psalmody and of the scriptural lessons was constantly interrupted and displaced. There was a considerable improvement with the new psalter and rubrics of 1911, but the Breviary still remained in need of reform: in 1971 the *Liturgia Horarum* was published as a replacement of the Roman Breviary, greatly simplifying and lightening the burden of the office and rationalising the psalter, the lectionary and the rubrics generally.

Since Newman's time, liturgical scholarship has shown that the continuous reading of scripture and the continuous recitation of the psalms were not features of the daily office in early times, but were monastic features grafted on the daily office of the Church as this office became thoroughly monasticised.[7]

Newman's remarks on the development of the Breviary were based mainly on three authorities: Gavanti's *Thesaurus Rituum*, Zaccaria's *Bibliotheca Ritualis*, and Palmer's *Origines Liturgicae*. Bartolomeo Gavanti (1569–1638) was a liturgical scholar who contributed to the reform of the Breviary undertaken by Clement VIII and Urban VIII. He published in 1628 his *Thesaurus sacrorum rituum, seu Commentaria in rubricis Missalis et Breviarii Romani*, a collection of material concerning the origins of the liturgy of the Western Church, together with a discussion of its supposed mystical significance. He belonged to the Clerks Regular of St Paul, founded in 1530, called 'Barnabites' from their headquarters at the church of St Barnabas in Milan. Francesco Antonio Zaccaria (1714–95) was a Jesuit scholar. His *Bibliotheca Ritualis* was published in Rome in two volumes in 1776 and 1781. William Palmer's *Origines Liturgicae* (first edition 1832, fourth edition 1845) was, as its sub-title indicates, a discussion of the 'Antiquities of the English Ritual and a Dissertation on Primitive Liturgies'. The opening

chapter of Volume 1 is devoted to the origins of Morning and Evening Prayer.

Some of the points made by Newman in the Tract would not be accepted without qualification today. His argument that there is scriptural warrant for prayer at the third, sixth and ninth hours among the Jews would not go unchallenged. The origins of Terce, Sext and None are now ascribed not to the supposed times of Jewish prayer but to the Roman divisions of the day. Furthermore it cannot be held that the Church developed seven canonical hours (counting Matins and Lauds as one), or alternatively seven day hours, in fulfilment of Verse 164 of Psalm 118(119). The supposed Jewish origins of the daily office and the influence of Jewish practices on the development of the office are now receiving considerable re-appraisal. Newman was not aware, of course, of the important distinction between the 'monastic' and 'cathedral' office. He does not mention the monastic origin of the offices of Prime and Compline, nor does he seem to have realised the extent to which the ancient Roman office came to be monasticised. Newman believed that the book known as the Breviary evolved as 'something between a directory and an harmony of offices': this would be generally supported by recent scholarship, but his subsequent suggestion that 'breviary' also implied abridgment or curtailment would need qualification. The Breviary was basically a conspectus and a unification of the various contents of the offices previously set out in separate volumes. Abridgment of the scriptural readings did unfortunately take place, but this was not due simply to the compilation of the Breviary but more importantly to other factors.

Newman gave a good account of Quiñonez's reform of the Breviary which had a considerable influence upon Cranmer, but he did not distinguish between the first and second recensions. He criticised the arrangement of scriptural passages and other unsatisfactory features of the Breviary along the lines of the preface to the Book of Common Prayer, which he sets in its historical context. The Roman Breviary in Newman's time still preserved the old Roman psalter. This was to be altered in 1911 when Pius X issued a new psalter and made some restoration of the temporal course of offices. Even so, there was still considerable scope for simplifying the Breviary, reducing the burden of offices for those not bound to choral recitation, and for restoring the liturgical character of the offices. The Prayer of the Church was still largely a clericalised institution. Newman also seemed to have accepted without criticism and as axiomatic the principles that the whole of the Bible should be read in the office in the course of each year and that all of the 150 psalms should be recited weekly, as in the Breviary, or monthly, as in the Prayer Book. These principles have been regarded as fundamental and self-evident ever since the office became monastic in character, and their application has bedevilled all attempts at reforming the daily prayer, both Roman and Anglican, right up to the present time. Despite the changes made in the *Liturgia Horarum* and the *Alternative Service Book*, the confusion concerning the function of the canonical offices has still not been entirely resolved: is it worship and praise? or personal edification? The latter view has tended to prevail and has been interpreted in terms of *lectio continua* and *recitatio continua*. On the other hand the former view is surely more correct, at least as regards the non-monastic use of the office, and on liturgical and pastoral grounds there is more to be said for a selective use of psalms and readings.

Newman did not view the breviary, as we might today, in the light of modern scholarship and contemporary liturgical thought. He wrote before the development of the Liturgical Movement and lacked many of its insights. He made certain important criticisms of the Breviary, and other criticisms which he at first thought important and then later abandoned. Otherwise, his approach to the Roman Breviary was characterised by respect, veneration and admiration. He saw it as one of the glories of the Western Church. Soon he saw an inconsistency between accepting the Breviary and rejecting Rome. But in the early and mid-thirties he still cherished the concept of the Church Catholic, which led him to suggest that the Church of

England should re-appropriate the Breviary. His love of the Breviary is summed up in the opening words of Tract 75:

> There is so much of excellence and beauty in the services of the Breviary, that were it skilfully set before the Protestant by Roman controversialists as the book of devotions received in their communion, it would undoubtedly raise a prejudice in their favour . . .

and the Tract was very influential in introducing the Church of England to a knowledge and use of the fuller daily office represented by the Roman Breviary.

The hymns of the breviary

The office hymn has been an established and important feature of the daily prayer of the Church in the West for many centuries. There were antecedents for both a daily form of prayer and for hymn singing from earlier times, but a recognisable daily office of a formalised kind cannot be identified before the fourth century. The introduction of the Latin office hymn in the West can be ascribed with certainty to Ambrose (c.339–397).[8] The vigils for which Ambrose wrote his first hymns were probably *ad hoc* services arranged during the persecution of the orthodox at Milan by Justina, mother of the Emperor Valentinian. They eventually became short vigil services held every night. There were also three daytime services in Ambrose's time at Milan, at morning, midday and evening. After Ambrose started writing hymns, they were introduced into the evening office, but there is no certainty when they were introduced into the other offices of the daytime. Ambrose soon had his imitators, and hymns written in his style were called *hymni ambrosiani.*

The use of the office hymn spread slowly and sporadically in Europe. These hymns were adopted more readily by monasteries and by centres such as Lérins and Arles where cathedrals and greater churches were influenced by monasteries. Caesarius, Benedict and Aurelian all provided for office hymns in their monastic rules. It was not until the twelth century that the hymn became a universal feature of the office in the West when it was at last admitted into the office of the Roman basilicas. Despite the slow progress made by the office hymn, the output of hymns in the Middle Ages was incredibly prolific. The monumental collection *Analecta Hymnica Medii Aevi*, compiled between 1886 and 1922 by Dreves, Blume and Bannister, ran to fifty-five volumes containing 28,296 items, of which 6,063 are hymns. Not all of these hymns were used in the office. Since the Middle Ages, further hymns have been composed. New offices have been added to the Roman Breviary with specially composed hymns, right up to the present time. Some fine hymns were composed for the Parisian Breviary, and these were greatly admired by Newman, Froude and other Tractarians. Since the Second Vatican Council, the Roman Breviary has been replaced by the *Liturgia Horarum* of 1971 which has forty-two newly composed hymns.[9]

The office hymn has a character of its own which distinguishes it from other hymns. It is traditionally laudal and proclamatory, rejoicing in, remembering, blessing and giving thanks for an aspect of the Christian mystery, either of time of day, or of season, or of feast. An authentic office hymn is distinctively liturgical, both as a composition and as an action performed by the people of God as part of the prayer of the Church. Newman seemed to have been attracted by the Latin office hymns because of their liturgical appropriateness. He seemed to be fascinated also by their Latinity, despite his fervent deprecation of their roughness of style in his two Prefaces to his Latin collections.

The Latin versions which Newman translated from the Roman Breviary were not, of course, the original versions. The version which appeared in the Roman Breviary in Newman's time was the 'corrected' version imposed on the Breviary by Urban VIII. Urban had ordered a thorough revision of the wording of the office hymns to remove what were then regarded as medieval crudities of style. The hymns were to be recast into a more classical mould. The revision was carried out relentlessly, and the four Jesuits entrusted with this task made 952 'corrections' in 81 of the 98 hymns. Some hymns were only slightly changed; others, such as the Advent hymn *Conditor alme siderum*, were almost completely rewritten. The new hymnal was published in 1629 and incorporated in the Roman Breviary in 1632 (though not in the 'exempt' breviaries such as the monastic: these retained the original texts). Despite constant criticism this corrected version remained the official text until the Roman Breviary was superseded by the *Liturgia Horarum* in 1971.

Newman played a leading part in introducing the nineteenth-century Church of England to office hymns. Cranmer himself had not been against office hymns as such and had indeed included them in his two projects for a reform of the Sarum Breviary. Their omission from the offices of the Book of Common Prayer was mainly due to Cranmer's own inability to translate Latin hymns into suitable English verse or to compose new hymns in the vernacular. It is doubtful, as Newman noted in one of his Prefaces, if there were any others capable of doing so at that time. It was only by the sixteenth century that it had become possible to compose a book of 'common' prayer in an English version which could be used and understood throughout the whole country. The English language had only recently become sufficiently developed for the composition of formal liturgical prose: it is doubtful whether an extensive vernacular hymnody for liturgical use would have been possible at that stage. In any case, Cranmer would have met with opposition from the Genevan party in the Church of England because of their dislike of church music in general. Perhaps, therefore, Cranmer had to decide also whether to follow Lutheranism in favouring hymns or Calvinism in excluding them.

William Drummond of Hawthornden is sometimes credited with being the first to compose acceptable translations of Latin hymns. However, it was not until the nineteenth century that there was any great development in this area. Newman was undoubtedly the chief pioneer in translating Latin hymns, although in fact he translated fewer hymns than some of the others who published translations. Chandler, Mant, and Isaac Williams were already working independently at translations, while Neale, Oakeley and Caswall were largely inspired to do so by Newman's example. The following list of the major publications at that time shows the growth of interest in translating Latin hymns, especially office hymns:

1836	Tract 75: 15 translations by Newman.
1837	John Chandler, *The Hymns of the Primitive Church, now first Collected, Translated and Arranged.* (80 hymns from the Parisian Breviary of 1736, 28 others.)
1837	Richard Mant, *Ancient Hymns from the Roman Breviary . . . to which are added Original Hymns.*
1839	Isaac Williams, *Hymns Translated from the Paris Breviary.*
1845	William Palmer (of Magdalen), *Short Poems and Hymns, the latter mainly translations.*
1848	William Copeland, *Hymns for the Week and Hymns for the Seasons. Translated from the Latin.*
1849	Edward Caswall, *Lyra Catholica, containing all the Breviary and Missal Hymns, with others from various sources.*
1851	John Mason Neale, *Hymni Ecclesiae e Breviariis Quibusdam et Missalibus Gallicanis, Germanis, Hispanis, Lusitanis Desumpti.*
1851, 1856	John Mason Neale, *Hymnal Noted.* Part I, 1851; Part II, 1856. (Neale was mainly responsible for the words. All the hymns are translations of hymns in general use in the Western Church before the reforms of Urban VIII. The English is in the same metre as the Latin.)

In time, English translations of Latin hymns were provided in various office books for use in the religious communities of the Church of England.[10] For these, Newman's translations were often used. In the Marquess of Bute's translation of the entire Roman Breviary, first published in 1879, all of Newman's and many of Caswall's translations were used. Some of Newman's translations began to appear in new hymnals. It is noteworthy that the first edition of *Hymns Ancient and Modern* (1861) contained 141 translations of Latin hymns, including one by Newman which has remained in all the subsequent editions: 'Come, Holy Ghost, who ever One' (*Nunc Sancte nobis Spiritus*). This hymn first appeared in Tract 75, but has received much editorial amendment since. In the early part of the twentieth century, Percy Dearmer did much to spread the use of liturgical hymns, many of them translations from the Latin, through the *English Hymnal* (1906) and *Songs of Praise* (1925). It can be said that although Newman translated only comparatively few Latin hymns, and that few of these have remained in constant use, he played a conspicuous part in encouraging the translation of Latin hymns and the use of genuinely liturgical hymns in the services of the Anglican and Roman Churches.

The Prefaces to Hymni Ecclesiae

It was a sign of Newman's continued interest in the Latin office hymns since the publication of Tract 75 in 1836 that he published in 1838 two collections of these hymns (Latin text only):

1. *Hymni Ecclesiae e Breviariis Romano, Sarisburiensi, Eboracensi et aliunde*. Oxford: J. H. Parker.
2. *Hymni Ecclesiae e Breviario Parisiensi*. Oxford: J. H. Parker.

Newman obviously wished to arouse interest among Anglicans in these hymns and especially in the concept of the office hymn. It is in this context that his willingness to contribute translations to the Breviary project attempted by Williams and Wood, the first phase of which took place in this same year, 1838, must be seen.

To the first of these collections Newman gave a Preface in Latin. This preface is best described as an apologia for publishing such a collection. He appealed in rather erudite Latin to the reader not to reject these hymns without a fair consideration. He did not deny the infelicities of style in some of the hymns: presumably Newman was aware that his readers would judge these hymns against the standards of classical poetry. He argued that what is old is not necessarily out of date, and that what is strange is not necessarily spurious. This unfortunately was the view of some of the reformers of the sixteenth century who undertook to revise the liturgy. Newman then made some strong criticisms of the English reformers: these criticisms were doubtless derived from Hurrell Froude. Newman may have written this preface in Latin to avoid making his views too conspicuous.

Newman went on to explain that the chief reason why there are no office hymns in the Book of Common Prayer was because there were no men in the sixteenth century with sufficient ability to provide suitable translations. At the same time, it seemed best to the reformers to cast aside the Latin hymns. He therefore offered these hymns to the judgment of his readers, assuring them that totally objectionable hymns (presumably those invoking the Saints or the Blessed Virgin Mary) had been omitted.

His preface to the other collection, hymns from the Parisian Breviary, was in English, and the style was warm and expansive compared with the cold and austere style of the Latin preface. He began with a comparison of psalms, the biblical canticles and hymns. The psalms and canticles were the result of inspiration, unlike the hymns, which were difficult to compose. Composing prayers is also difficult because one is addressing Almighty God. The difficulty of composing prayers had been overcome, Newman argued, to a great extent by the use of Sentences, taken from the scriptures; by repeating the Lord's Prayer and the *Kyrie Eleison*; and by the use of the collect form, as collects 'lessen the difficulty of addressing God by subjecting it to fixed rules'. Part of the success of the collect form is brevity and conciseness: long public prayers are usually unsuitable, whereas successful prayers are usually brief. Newman then referred to the eucharistic prayer as being one of the few successful long prayers:

> The great Eucharistic Prayer is nearly the only long prayer in the Catholic Church: and there is every reason to suppose that in its substance it proceeds from inspired authorities.

His next sentence was probably inspired by Hurrell Froude's Tract 63: 'In our own Services it has been separated by our Reformers into three distinct portions.'

Newman went on to discuss the difficulties involved in composing hymns and remarked that the Church of England with 'remarkable caution which she displays so often' had not attempted to provide office hymns. She rejected the Roman hymns and substituted in their place not vernacular hymns but metrical psalms. The lack of office hymns had led to some Anglicans supplying unsuitable hymns in their place: but Newman warned that one must wait until the time was ripe for suitable hymns to be composed: 'This is the proper answer to inconsiderate complaints and impatient interference.' The next sentence might almost have been written a century and a half later: 'There have before now been divines who could write a Liturgy in thirty-six hours. Such is not our Church's way.' This preface is more tactful and conciliatory, and less critical of the Church of England and the reformation, than the Latin preface.

Newman concluded with an interesting discussion of the merits of the Latin hymns, and suggested that

> thoughtful minds naturally revert to the discarded collections of the ante-reform era, discarded because of associations with which they were then viewed, and of the interpolations by which they were disfigured; but which, when purified from these, are far more profitable to the Christian than the light and wanton effusions which are their present substitute among us.

These merits are to be found even in the hymns from the comparatively modern Parisian Breviary, which he now recommended to his readers. As before, he was at pains to point out that hymns containing invocations to the Saints had been omitted.

In neither of these prefaces did Newman advocate the actual use of these hymns by Anglicans either in private devotion or in the Prayer Book offices. Probably he published them in the first place because he had grown to love these Latin hymns and thought it was likely that others would come to like them if they were made available. Perhaps also he hoped to dissipate some of the prejudice against the Roman liturgy by revealing some of the literary and spiritual riches it contained – a continuation of his avowed aim in Tract 75. Others were also working at this. The previous year John Chandler's *Hymns of the Primitive Church* had appeared. Despite the title, most of the hymns were from the Parisian Breviary. Chandler provided both the original texts and some verse translations. In the following year Isaac Williams published *Hymns translated from the Paris Breviary*.

It may seem strange that in the same year that he published these two collections of Latin hymns, each supported by eloquent recommendations, Newman was giving qualified support to Robert Williams and Samuel Wood in their translation project, and eventually brought about its abandonment. His misgivings arose from considerations of prudence, however; he had not lost his love of the Breviary and its hymns.

Newman's translations of Latin office hymns

Newman made a total of forty-seven translations of Latin office hymns (see Chapter Eleven). For convenience the hymns are referred to by the number assigned to each one in the list. The translations may be divided into the three stages in which they were produced:

1. Newman began with twelve translations made for Tract 75, first published in 1836. He translated the hymns for a Sunday in Summertime (2, 4–8, 21, 28), for the feast of the Transfiguration (32, 33), and from the Common of a Martyr for the feast of St Laurence (34, 35).
2. He later made thirty-three translations for the Breviary translation project of Robert Williams and Samuel Wood in

1838. From the notebooks in which he entered these translations (see below) we know which hymns he translated for this purpose, namely those required for the Psalter (in addition to the Sunday hymns already translated for Tract 75) (1, 3, 9–20, 22–27) and for propers in the Pars Hiemalis (Advent 29–31, Christmastide 38–43, Lent 44–45).

Finally in this group were his translations of *Stabat Mater dolorosa* and *Tristes erant apostoli* (36, 37), composed possibly, though not certainly, for future use in the translation of the Breviary.

3. The third group consists of two translations made at Littlemore in 1842 from the Parisian Breviary, namely the hymn for Prime and the hymn *Christe Pastorum* from the Common of a Confessor Bishop (46, 47).

In the section of the Breviary translation by Williams and Wood which was actually printed are to be found Newman's translations of the hymns *per annum* in the Psalter (1–28) and the hymns for Advent (29, 30, 31). Newman made ten further translations for this translation: these are in his manuscript notebooks and have not hitherto been published (36–45). (See Chapter Ten.)

In his collected verse, *Verses on Various Occasions*, first published in 1867, Newman included thirty-five of his translations. (See Chapter Eleven.) All of these, except the two hymns from the Parisian Breviary, were used by the Marquess of Bute in his English translation of the Roman Breviary. He also used Newman's translation of the hymn for Prime which is in Tract 75.[11]

Among Newman's manuscripts at the Birmingham Oratory are two bound notebooks in which Newman wrote his translations made for the Breviary translation project. The notebooks are inscribed 'John H. Newman, Trinity College, 1818' and had remained unused since that time.[12] As he added the date on which he completed each hymn, it is possible to trace in detail his progress in translating these hymns for Williams and Wood.

He began by translating the hymns for the days of the week

per annum as these would be the first items required by the translators. Although the *Pars Hiemalis* of the Roman Breviary commenced with the beginning of Advent, the volume opened with the Psalter in which the hymns per annum were included, being required in the time between Epiphany and Lent. The first translation, of the hymn for Matins for Sunday in wintertime, was marked 7 March 1837. It is not known why he made this isolated translation at this date: perhaps he was considering making his own translation of the Breviary. The remaining hymns are all dated 1838. They consist of the Matins hymns for Monday (18 February), Tuesday (23 February), Wednesday (8 March), Thursday (14 March), Friday (15 March), Saturday (19 March); the Lauds hymns for Sunday (wintertime) (21 March), Monday (26 March), Tuesday (29 March), Wednesday (31 March), Thursday (2 April), Friday (5 April), Saturday (5 April); Vespers hymns for Monday (8 April), Tuesday (10 April), Wednesday (12 April), Thursday (13 April – 'Good Friday'), Friday (13 April), and Saturday (14 April – 'Sabbato Sancto'). The hymns for Sunday Vespers, the four Little Hours and Compline had already been translated for Tract 75.

In the other notebook, he began with a translation of the *Stabat Mater dolorosa* lines 1–24 (May 1838). In Newman's time the Feast of the Seven Sorrows of BVM was celebrated on the Friday after Passion Sunday. The second hymn was a translation of *Tristes erant apostoli* for Vespers, Common of Apostles in Paschaltide (May 1838). Presumably these were translated with the project in mind, though they were rather randomly selected and would not have been required for a long time. Perhaps Newman made these translations because these hymns appealed to him. Then occurs his Advent hymns for Vespers (5 September), Matins (7 September) and Lauds (3 October). After this, there are new translations, the hymns for Christmas Vespers (9 October) and Lauds (11 October), both with considerable alterations in the manuscript; for Holy Innocents Matins (12 October) and Lauds (13 October); for Epiphany Vespers (14 October) and Lauds (16 October); and for Sundays in Lent, Vespers (17 October) and Matins (26 October). By the end of 1838 the project had been called off, and Newman did not compose any more translations for Williams and Wood.

Parochial Sermon: The Daily Service[13]

On Monday, 30 June 1834, Newman began the practice of reading Morning Prayer daily in St Mary's Church. After the opening of the Church of St Mary the Virgin and St Nicholas in 1836, Evening Prayer was read daily in Littlemore. Newman wrote to Froude on 21 June 1834:

> Further, I think I mean on St. Peter's day, i.e. next Sunday, to announce my intention of reading the morning service daily in the chancel while and whenever I am in Oxford, *according* to the injunction of the Church, whether people attend or not. I shall have a desk put up near the altar, facing the south, from which I shall read the Psalms and Lessons, kneeling, however, towards the east. It seems to me that the absurdity, as it appears to many, of Tom Keble's daily plan is, his praying to *empty benches*. Put yourself near the altar, and you may be solitary. I see this agrees with a notion of yours. I am the more eager to begin this service because the Provost pointedly refused to let me keep open the chapel at Christmas (N.B. – though I was Dean). I have waited long enough to show that I am not acting from 'irritation'.[14]

Despite the injunction in the Prayer Book, few churches at that time celebrated the daily offices, and Newman's action would have appeared a strange innovation to many. By coincidence, the day after the above letter to Froude was written, the Rev R. F. Wilson wrote to Newman:

> I have been much surprised to find an injunction in the preface to the prayer Book, to the effect that all priests and deacons are to say daily the morning and evening prayers, either privately or openly, not being let by sickness or other urgent cause. Do you consider this binding?[15]

Newman did, of course, take the injunction seriously: he

professed complete loyalty to the Prayer Book and this doubtless weighed heavily with him in deciding to read morning prayer daily in church. At the same time it can be inferred from his arguments in this sermon, and from what is known of his general development, that liturgical reasons were also important to him, or at least were beginning to be important.

The decision was also influenced to some extent by Isaac Williams who had recently become Newman's curate. Williams seems to have taken all the credit to himself for this development at St Mary's, to judge from a passage in his *Autobiography*:

> Thomas Keble had resolved, about 1816, when he made that collection of 'Authorities for the use of the Daily Service' published in the *Tracts for the Times*,[16] that, if he ever had a parish of his own, he would at once begin daily service, which he did immediately on coming to reside at Bisley in 1827.
>
> This was the origin of the revival of the daily service. The Kebles at Fairford were in the habit of reading the daily Church service in their family; and when Thomas Keble (in the year 1827) had the living of Bisley given him, then in lieu of the prayer meetings which had been customary in that parish, he established the daily service in the church, which was then spoken of as a strange fancy. Having been therefore long accustomed to this, when I first became Newman's curate at St. Mary's, in common with a great many less definite opinions and practices which I imported from Bisley, one was a daily morning service at St. Mary's, to which we afterwards added this service at Littlemore in the afternoon, so that there should be both services daily in the parish. It was from this that the custom had since prevailed throughout the kingdom.[17]

The church at Littlemore was completed in 1836 and consecrated in September of that year. Isaac Williams wrote:

> It was considered quite a model of a church at the time, though built hastily. Oakridge Church, in Bisley parish, which was being built at the same time, with so much more caution and care, was comparatively a failure. So much was it Newman's way to do things quickly and successfully. I was appointed the curate of Littlemore, and as we had the daily service there every afternoon, it was the

> constant walk of Newman and myself. I had lodgings there and spent the Sundays and Saints' days at Littlemore.[18]

Newman preached his sermon 'The Daily Service' in St Mary's on 2 November 1834. It was a parochial sermon, not a university sermon. The daily recitation of Morning Prayer had by then been established for four months. Newman began the sermon with some reflections on biblical texts on prayer. He then appealed to the practice of the primitive Church, giving considerable detail about the practices of early Christians. This he did in a simple fashion without turning the sermon into a learned discourse. It is tempting to see some of this material as foreshadowing Tract 75; however, it is clear that he did not take any interest in the Breviary until after Froude's death. His main concern at this stage was two-fold: the importance of obeying the Prayer Book injunction and the value of corporate prayer. Corporate prayer has a value not possessed by private prayer, even if the group be small. This prayer, he argued, would be to the good of all the parish, not only for those present. Those who were not present could turn their thoughts to God at that hour, uniting themselves in spirit with the act of corporate prayer. The main thrust of this sermon, therefore, was pastoral and spiritual.

CHAPTER NINE

Outcome: 'This is *a Religion'*

The part played in Newman's conversion by his understanding of the liturgy, and especially by his encounter with the Roman Breviary, can only be understood in terms of his developing ecclesiology. In the *Apologia* Newman recalled the widespread belief that he was already a crypto-Roman Catholic[1] There was in fact little or nothing to predispose Newman to have any liking for the Church of Rome. For much of his Anglican life and in common with most Anglicans, Newman was influenced by 'ingrained fears of Rome'[2] and associated that church with anti-Christ. Yet in spite of these fears, he had felt in 1841 a 'secret longing love of Rome the Mother of English Christianity'.[3]

He was not yet ready to dissociate Rome from this maternal relationship. Despite painful disillusionment with the Anglican Church it still bound him with deep ties and there were difficulties about Rome which had to be overcome. Even in 1844, a year of darkness for Newman, he still believed in his Anglican orders.[4] Rome was still quite unattractive, at least in her externals. 'I am setting my face absolutely towards the wilderness', he wrote to Keble in November 1844, and in the following month, 'No one can have a more unfavourable view than I of the present state of the Roman Catholics.'[5]

Newman's journey towards rejection of the English Church and acceptance of Rome had been in three phases, and these were overlapping rather than sequential. The first was his search for the identity of the Church of England. In his early days at Oriel, his embryonic attempts at an ecclesiology had led him to see the Church not as a human institution but a divinely founded body. All his life he was deeply committed to the cause of revealed religion, fundamental to which was the dogmatic principle. He constantly emphasised in his Anglican sermons the indwelling in the soul of the Holy Spirit and the presence of Christ in the Church. The newly-discovered reality of the Incarnation and his conversion to belief in baptismal regeneration entailed for him a view of the Church as an integrated body, with a definite structure and organisation. He insisted upon the divine origin of the Church, its foundations upon the apostles, and its incarnational character. The Church had authority to teach and a commission to dispense the sacramental grace by which the supernatural life gained in baptism is sustained in the soul. Newman wholeheartedly followed in his own life the gospel ideal of holiness, and the same ideal figured largely in his view of the Church. Holiness was one of the four 'notes' of the Church, and one of her chief tasks was the fostering of holiness in her members.[6] Such a Church had to be a unitary body: it could not consist of various bodies joined only with the loosest of ties. Having arrived at the notion of the Church Catholic, Newman concluded that the Anglican Church must be the Church Catholic in England. If the Church of England did not look like part of the Church Catholic, then it had lost sight of its true nature. At this stage in his development, Newman could not and did not conceive of any other candidate for the position of the Church Catholic in England: it could not be any other than the Church of England. With new-found confidence, he set out to restore to the church of his birth a realisation of its catholicity. He helped to formulate the claims of the early Tractarian programme and pursued them enthusiastically.

The second phase of his journey now began. He had staked out a position for the Church of England to occupy. He soon found that the bishops and a greater part of the clergy and people were opposed to seeing themselves as a part of the Church Catholic. Newman began to understand that it is one thing to form a concept of the Church Catholic and to assume that the Church of England was synonymous with it: it was quite another matter to show that this was the correct identity of the Church of England. His study of the Fathers of the Church and his acquaintance with the Anglican divines enabled him to build up a profile of the true Church as sacramental and fundamentally liturgical. At first he was able to see the Anglican Church as simply having lost sight of its catholicity: in which case, a programme of renewal, such as that proposed by the Tractarians, was required. But as he studied the early history of the Church, and especially as he gained from the patristic writings an insight into the early heresies, doubts began to grow about the logical possibility of the Anglican Church being a branch of the Church Catholic.

His optimism received two sharp blows in 1839. During the long vacation he studied the history of the Church in the fifth century. He noted that the extreme Monophysites led by Eutyches were condemned at the Council of Chalcedon. His attention was then arrested by the growth of the moderate Monophysite party. This party, which became very strong in the Eastern Church, rejected the Eutychean position without accepting in full the decisions of the Council of Chalcedon. Here surely was a prototype of a *via media* church, and yet they were considered heretics along with the Eutycheans. On this analogy then both the Church of England, which prided itself on its *via media* position, and the Protestants were equally heretical. The weakness of the *via media* position, on which Newman had hitherto set much store, now began to be apparent. However much such a Church kept close to orthodoxy, it still remained outside the Church Catholic. Its detachment meant isolation. Unsupported by the Church Catholic, from whom it was cut off, it could not claim to derive or share in any of the authority of that Church. In Newman's ecclesiology there must be a lineal descent of authority based on the apostolic succession. On this view, a *via media* Church is self-authenticating. The claim of some of the Tractarians that the Church of England had been cut off from the main body of the Church Catholic through no fault of its own no longer seemed so valid. It seemed to be more the case that the Anglican

Church did not have the link with the universal Church which Newman would have wished for it.

Furthermore Newman began to see what was implied by specifying obedience to Chalcedon as the bedrock of faith. If Chalcedon was authoritative, so was Trent. The eclecticism of a *via media* becomes self-defeating. His doubts were redoubled when he read Wiseman's article in the *Dublin Review*, 'The Anglican Claim to Apostolical Succession'. He was impressed not so much by the supposed parallel between Donatists and Anglicans as by Augustine's appeal to the general consent of Christians summed up in the dictum *securus judicat orbis terrarum*. What had been intended by the Tractarians as a defence of the Church of England from state encroachment by appealing to the autonomy of the Church Catholic now only served to show the isolation of the Church of England.

Newman's confidence in the Anglican Church was now badly shaken, although he managed to reassure himself for the time being. The branch theory no longer seemed tenable and it gave no status to his church. The *via media* doctrine now appeared to be equally meaningless: there never had been a *via media* church at any time in history, and it was simply a 'paper doctrine'. The rejection by the Anglican bishops and most of their flock of Newman's claims for Catholicity indicated that both these doctrines were mistaken. Newman had been particularly shaken by the bishops' condemnation of Tract 90 in their charges. His arguments were not given the serious attention they deserved, and, much misunderstood, the Tract completely failed in its irenical purpose. Reluctantly he began to grasp the cruel conclusion to which events were drawing him, that the English Church lacked, not only in practice but, more significantly, in principle, the traditional 'notes' of the Church Catholic.

He now entered the third phase of the journey. His view of the Church of England was undermined, but this did not immediately lead him Romewards. A further path was still before him: he had to seek authentication for the Church of Rome, a task he approached with a heavy heart. Apart from his natural reluctance to countenance any move towards Rome, there were seemingly insuperable difficulties. If Canterbury was in default by its rejection of authority derived from the apostolic succession, then by the same token Rome was guilty of departing from this authority in as much as it had added to the Faith. 'Does the Church ... know more now than the Apostles knew?', Newman asked in a response to Wiseman written the following year (1840).[7] For him 'the faith of Rome is an addition to the primitive', and he resisted the claim of the Romanists that their so-called additions were developments of revelation. Developments were no more acceptable than additions.

For some two years, he continued in the assertion he had made in response to Wiseman that 'there is sufficient ground for still believing that the English Church is at this time the Catholic Church in England'.[8] However, during the summer of 1841 Newman was translating the treatises of Athanasius against Arius and he was struck by the parallel between the Arian controversy and the Monophysite. In this instance the Arians were comparable to Protestants, the semi-Arians were like the Anglicans in holding to a *via media* position, and again 'Rome now was what it was then': to Newman, 'the ghost had come a second time'.[9] He continued to maintain his Anglican stance in his sermons and in Tract 90. The latter convinced many that he was now firmly set in a Romeward direction, and yet he wrote it to hold others, and perhaps himself, back from Rome. In the summer of 1843 he came to realise how he really stood and told Keble in a letter 'I consider the Roman Catholic Communion the Church of the Apostles, and that what grace is among us (which, through God's mercy, is not little) is extraordinary ...'[10] He could not fully accept the feasibility of the development of doctrine, although he was moving towards it, so he set himself to work out the theory in a book. Before he had finished writing the final section of *An Essay on the Development of Christian Doctrine* all his difficulties with the notion of development were resolved and nothing then stood in the way of his submission to Rome.

Newman held what might be called a holistic view of the

Church. Its structure was not arbitrary, but the result of divine foundation and design. He conceived it as an integrated body, made up of interrelated elements, one of the most important of which was the sacramental principle. As we saw earlier, he came to realise the significance of the sacraments in the life of the Church at an early stage in his development. From his reading of the Fathers he was doubtless familiar with the Augustinian dictum that 'the Eucharist makes the Church'. The spirit of this dictum, extended to all the sacraments of the Church, is implicit in his thought. In the sacraments, man worships God and receives God's gift of grace. Hence worship in the forms required by the Eucharist and the sacramental rites is intrinsic to a Catholic view of the Church. For this reason, there was a liturgical dimension in Newman's developing ecclesiology.

Newman's thought in many ways foreshadowed the teachings of the Second Vatican Council. The place of the laity in the Church, the supremacy of conscience, the Church as a communion of all its members, a renewed emphasis on scripture and the Fathers of the Church, a commitment to Christian unity, and the call of the whole Church to evangelisation were themes of the Council which owed much to the influence of Newman. Both in the Anglican and in the Catholic Church, Newman saw the need for the Church to meet the needs of the age and thereby to regain her rightful place in the modern world. This, too, was the spirit of the Council. It was an outstanding principle of Newman's pastoral practice at St Clement's, St Mary's, and Littlemore that the Holy Communion, the sacraments and the daily office were of primary importance in the life of the Church. He saw the liturgy as being at the heart of the Church, and the explicit development of this view was one of the chief achievements of the Second Vatican Council.

Speaking of the essential place of the liturgy in the Church, the Council declared:

> It is through the liturgy, especially the divine Eucharistic Sacrifice, that the work of our redemption is exercised. The liturgy is thus the

> outstanding means by which the faithful can express in their lives, and manifest to others, the mystery of Christ and the real nature of the true Church ... Day by day the liturgy builds up those within the Church into the Lord's holy temple ... To outsiders the liturgy reveals the Church as a sign raised above the nations.[11]

Although Newman did not articulate his beliefs on the liturgy as explicitly as this, the spirit of this teaching was adumbrated in his sermons. For him the Church had been founded as a worshipping Church: the Church Catholic was necessarily sacramental and liturgical by nature. One of the central criteria he applied in authenticating a church was the quality of its worship: hence his desire to restore the full observance of the Prayer Book. At first this was sufficient: he saw his Church as possessing full authority, and therefore its Prayer Book was authoritative. Gradually, as we have seen, he progressed to a fuller expectation of what the Church's liturgy comprised. As he developed a sense of the liturgy, he came to see not only the origins of the Prayer Book but also its limitations. Influenced in varying degrees by Froude, Lloyd, Palmer, Keble and Pusey, he came to have a more profound understanding of the liturgical basis of the Church. He came to realise, probably from Froude's Tract 63, the traditional structure of the eucharistic prayers of East and West. He began to understand more clearly that the Church of Rome had preserved and maintained the fullness of the Eucharist, whatever devotional excesses may have accrued to its celebration.

Liturgical considerations were beginning to influence his attitude towards Rome as the Tractarian movement got under way and as he picked up more knowledge of the Roman liturgy from Froude and others. There was a decisive step forward when Newman, at the fortuitous suggestion of Rogers, acquired Froude's breviary. For the first time, he studied the Roman offices in detail and came to admire them. As a result he began to recite the offices. Henceforth the Breviary was significant to him, playing a formative part in his development. It proved to be both an impressive and a disturbing influence in his life. It was disturbing because the translation projects increasingly caused controversy among his colleagues in the Tractarian movement. It was even more disturbing because it led him to see the Church of Rome in a different light. It opened a window on to that church through which he was drawn to study her more penetratingly than ever before. It was as if he came to think that the Church possessed a special character, despite her objectionable externals, if her spirituality was that reflected in the breviary.

His encounter with the Breviary provided Newman with his first opportunity to 'get on the inside' of the Roman liturgy and to make a detailed study of a liturgical book. He found it, by comparison with the Prayer Book, greatly enriched both devotionally and liturgically. There were many features in the Breviary which appealed strongly to him. In the Breviary offices the whole of the psalter was prayed weekly and enriched with antiphons; almost the whole of scripture was read at Matins (or would have been if the *lectio continua* had not been disrupted by the overloading of saints' feasts with their own propers); and the homilectic lessons at Matins provided a daily reading from the Fathers. The hagiographical lessons, although badly in need of revision, gave an insight into the history and the spirituality of the Church. The course of the Breviary offices throughout the year celebrated with considerable richness both the liturgical seasons and ordinary time, together with other feasts of the Lord, the Virgin Mary and the saints. The time of day was also sanctified by the daily round of offices. Antiphons, versicles and responsories all served to enrich the liturgical prayer of the Breviary. Above all Newman was impressed by the office hymns.

His growing sense of liturgy, both in its Anglican and in its Roman manifestations, enhanced his conceptualisation of the Church Catholic. He had grasped the fundamental connection between the Church's liturgical worship and her identity as a church. Implicit in his thought was the notion that the liturgy is constitutive of the Church Catholic. Implicit also was the spirit of the maxim *Lex orandi, lex credendi.* Newman was highly sensitive to the way in which the faith of the Church had developed systematically. Part of this development is related to the liturgy, and there is a constant interaction between liturgy and faith: the prayer of the Church informs the development of faith, and the faith shapes the liturgy. The notion that the law of prayer is the law of belief assigns a significant priority to liturgy: it is a normative function of liturgical prayer to shape belief. Liturgical theology in the twentieth century has returned to this way of seeing the importance of liturgy in the life of the Church. Early-nineteenth-century writers on liturgy did not develop this aspect of liturgical theology, and it was not discussed specifically by Newman. What Newman did say in his sermons and writings about liturgical worship is highly consistent with this stance, however, and the liturgy, together with the main liturgical books, was a *locus theologicus* of considerable significance for his developing ecclesiology.

The Roman liturgy, and especially the Breviary, was a decisive factor in Newman's journey towards Rome, a factor which has not received due attention in the corpus of literature dealing with his conversion. Newman encountered the Breviary almost by accident. Its influence on him, continuing perhaps the influence of his friend Hurrell Froude, must not be underestimated. He became almost captivated by this book and could not put it aside. Despite the ill-feeling caused by the abortive Breviary translation projects, despite his discouragement of others from using the Breviary if it turned them Romewards, despite his painful realisation that it was drawing him towards Rome, he continued to pray the offices. Wisely or unwisely he took the bold step of reciting the offices daily with his companions at Littlemore, despite his desire to hold them back from Rome. The Breviary continued to have a fascination for him, and it is fitting that it featured at the very end of his journey to Rome.

At the height of the Tractarian movement, Newman would probably have concurred with Palmer in seeing a continuity between the Catholic and Anglican liturgies. By the Littlemore period, however, he was probably more aware (in the spirit of Froude's Tract 63) of the discontinuity. Cranmer's offices in the

Prayer Book were a very attenuated version of the incomparable Breviary offices. With the Breviary as his daily prayer he had come with anguish to identify the church which had given birth to this prayer book as the Church of the Apostles. Liturgy counted for something as he examined the identity first of the Church of England and then of the Church of Rome. In his day the former could not be persuaded to take up the authority, the apostolicity, and the liturgy which would have pertained to the catholicity which Newman once claimed for it. Rome for all its outward defects had retained all these, including a fully developed liturgy. As Newman wrote in the *Apologia*:

> While I had confidence in the *via media,* and thought that nothing could overset it, I did not mind laying down large principles, which I saw would go further than was commonly perceived. I considered that to make the *via media* concrete and substantive, it must be much more than it was in outline; that the Anglican Church must have a ceremonial, a ritual, and a fulness of doctrine, which it had not at present, if it were to compete with the Roman Church with any prospect of success.[12]

But the English Church at that time had neither the liturgy nor the doctrine:

> I looked at her [the Catholic Church]; at her rites, her ceremonial, and her precepts; and I said 'This *is* a religion'; and then, when I looked back upon the poor Anglican Church, for which I had laboured so hard, and upon all that appertained to it, and thought of our various attempts to dress it up doctrinally and aesthetically, it seemed to me to be the veriest of nonentities.[13]

PART TWO
Newman's Translations

CHAPTER TEN

Ten Translations

The ten translations which make up this chapter have not been published before. Newman composed a total of forty-seven translations of Latin office hymns. The ten hitherto unpublished, numbered 36 to 45 in the annotated list given in Chapter Eleven, were intended for the translation of the Roman Breviary. They were not used as the project was eventually abandoned, but remained in two manuscript notebooks. Composed by Newman in 1838 (mostly in October) during the first phase of the translation project, they consist of the hymns for Christmas, Holy Innocents, Epiphany, and Lent, and two others.[1]

36.
Stabat mater
(Seven Sorrows of the B.V.M.)

Cheerlessly and tearfully
Stood the dolorous Mother nigh
  To the Cross that bore her Son;
And her soul was sore bestead
Sank with Him, and with Him bled,
  For a sword had through it gone.

O how sad and melancholy
Seemed she then, that Mother holy
  Of the Father's Onlyborn;
Who was sighing and was tearful
And did tremble at the fearful
  Pains with which her Son was torn.

Who could see her and not weep
Christ's own Mother in so deep
   And so bitter punishment?
Whose the heart but would condole
With that Mother's tender soul
   In her Son's afflictions rent?

For She saw Him tortured
By the scourge and cross, instead
   Of His people sunk and lost;
For She saw her sweet firstborn
In the throes of death forlorn
   Giving up at length the ghost.

37.
Commune Apostolorum
(In Tempore Paschali)
Vespers

Deep in despair the Apostles were
   When on that bitter day
The people rose, their Master's foes,
   And bore His life away.

What did ensue, the Angel twice
   Unto the women told;
Next Christ Himself by voice and view
   Showed to His faithful fold.

With the glad news the eleven to greet
   The women hasten home;
And Him they meet, and clasp His sweet
   And shining feet, o'ercome.

The Apostles speed, where He doth lead
   To the Galilean height;
And there upon His gifts they feed,
   And triumph in His light.

That it may bide, this Easter tide,
Within us through the year,
From sin's fresh grave Thy people save,
Once raised, Redeemer dear.

To Father praise be paid always
And praise be to the Son,
Who once was slain, then rose again,
And Spirit, Three in One.

38.
Christmas
Vespers

Saviour of souls undone,
Who, ere the birth of light,
Wast ever the Co-equal Son
Of the Dread Infinite.

The Father's Image bright,
Man's never failing stay,
Lord, look upon the hearts contrite,
Where'er Thy servants pray.

Remember how of old,
Born of the Virgin's womb,
Thou didst put on our earthly mould,
Creator, and didst come.

The Day again is here,
When erst Thou didst resign
Thy Father's bosom and appear
Earth's only medicine.

The Day, which earth, sea, sky
And firmament above,
Hail for the health it brought, and cry
With a new strain of love.

We whom the sacred dews
Of Thy blest flood assay,
Will echo back the eternal news
In token of Thy Day.

Jesu! all praise be Thine,
Thou whom the Virgin bore,
With Father and with Spirit divine,
Now and for evermore.

39.
Christmas Lauds

From the rising of the day
To its setting far away,
Sing we Christ, this holy morn,
Of the Virgin Mary born.

Of the new world Author blest
He in a slave's garb has drest,
So by flesh the flesh to aid,
Lest He lose whom He had made.

Heavenly grace has found a home
In the undefiled Mother's womb,
And she bears a secret blessing,
Knowing nought yet all possessing.

That chaste bosom doth enshrine
Suddenly a guest divine;
And her virgin loneliness
Thrills at a sweet son's caress.

Till her very arms enfold
Him whom Gabriel's voice foretold,
Whom the Baptist had adored
Ere his birth – his hidden Lord.

In a manger next He lay
Pleased to slumber mid the hay;
Fed on milk, His frugal fare,
Who sustains the birds of air.

Then the choirs celestial sing,
And the Angels to their King;
And to shepherds in the field
The Eternal Master is revealed.

Jesu, whom the Virgin bore,
Praise be thine for evermore,
Praise unto the Father be
And the Spirit, One and Three.

40.
Holy Innocents
Matins

The jealous king is told
  The King of Kings is come,
Who claims the right of Israel's fold,
  And David's royal home.

'A rival fills the throne,'
  He cries in frantic mood,
'Take arms, my soldier, and be gone,
  The cradles bathe in blood.'

What boots the cruel deed?
  And what is its return?
That child escapes – the rest may bleed –
  Over their bodies borne.
(Doxology as at Christmas Vespers)

41.
Holy Innocents
Lauds

Blossoms of the martyr band
By the fell Christ-hating hand
Snatches away in dawning light
As rosebuds by the tempest's might.

First for Christ to shed your life,
Tender flock for slaughterer's knife,
Neath the altar blithe and gay
With your palms and crown ye play.

Jesu, whom the Virgin bore, etc.

42.
Epiphany
Vespers

Why fear thy God should come,
  Tyrant, to reign below?
He will not mortal pomp assume
  Who can a heaven bestow.

A star goes on before,
  Long ways the Magians trod.
Light leads to Light, and they adore
  With gifts the present God.

By Jordan's lucid tides
  A heavenly Lamb is seen;
No guilt He brings, but ours abides,
  Washing the sinner clean.

New prodigy divine!
  The water pots grow red;
The stream, when bid, flows forth in wine,
  Disowns its river head.

Jesu, whom love displays
To heathen tribes thy face,
To Father and to Thee be praise
And to the Spirit of Grace.

43.
Epiphany
Lauds

Greater far than cities great,
Bethlehem! thou art the gate
Of the High Deliverer come
From heaven to make the flesh His home.

While a softer gleaming star
Than the sun and brighter far
Tells to earthly ears the birth
Of God in the attire of earth.

Magians see Him, and they bring
Their choice eastern offering.
And with suppliant knee unfold
Myrrh, and frankincense, and gold.

Gold a Monarch to declare,
Frankincense that God is there,
Myrrh to tell the heavier tale
Of His tomb and funeral.

Jesu, praise to Thee be paid
Who to heathen art displayed,
To the Father, as is meet,
And the Holy Paraclete.

44.
Lent
Vespers

Who hast the world's foundations cast,
Hear Thou the prayers and weepings sore
Which in this sacred fast
Of forty days we pour.

Thou who dost search yet spare the heart,
Canst tell how poor and weak our best,
To penitent impart
The grace of pardon blest.

Heinous in sooth our sin and shame,
Yet pity the confessing tongue;
And glorify Thy name
By healing the unstrung.

Bruise Thou our flesh with abstinence,
Until our hearts be spare from sin,
Nor feed on the gross sense
Of evil stored within.

List Holy One, grant blessed Three,
That these our duties stern and high
Of Lent may fruitful be
To absolve and purify.

45.
Lent
Matins

Taught in the ancient mystic rite
Let us observe this Lent,
To fast and pray with hearts contrite
For forty days content.

The Law and Prophets in their day
  Set forth the solemn rule,
Then Christ, who time doth make and sway,
  And came when time was full.

So let us stint our food and sleep,
  Our thoughts and jests which rise
In converse free, and duly keep
  Our watch in stricter wise.

And shun the mischief that beguiles
  And slays the truant soul,
And foil our adversary's wiles
  And tyrannous control.

And soothe the wrath which burns so high,
  And sue the judgment just,
And pour our supplicatory cry,
  And grovel in the dust.

We sin, O God, and try full sore
  Thy everlasting love;
Yet, Lord of grace, still let it pour
  In pardon from above.

Remember, Lord, our first estate,
  A mortal work, but Thine;
Nor let another arrogate
  What bears the Name Divine.

Undo the evil we have done,
  The good we ask fulfil;
That we, while endless ages run,
  Henceforth may please Thee still.

Grant Holy One and Blessed Three,
  Our duties high and stern
Of the long Lent may fruitful be
  To cleanse the heart and turn.

CHAPTER ELEVEN

Notes on the Translations

Newman made forty-seven translations of Latin Office Hymns, thirty-seven of which were published. This chapter gives a full annotated list of all forty-seven. The hymns are numbered in one sequence and the translations divided into Sections 1 to 4.

In the first three sections, the office (as in pre-1911 editions of the Roman Breviary) is indicated in which the hymn was used, followed by the first line of the English translation. The first line of the Latin version is then given. This version represents the 'corrections' made by Urban VIII. Where the first line differs from that of the original, the latter is given in parentheses. The authorship of the hymn is given where this is known.

Abbreviations have been used throughout this chapter and are clarified below:

AH	Indicates that the original version of the hymn may be consulted in the standard work of reference for Latin hymns of the Middle Ages, *Analecta Hymnica Medii Aevi.*[1] The reference is to volume and page.
LH	Indicates that the hymn, using the original Latin version, sometimes with editorial amendments, has been used in the *Liturgia Horarum* (1971) which has now superseded the *Breviarium Romanum.*[2] The reference given is to volume and page.
Brev. Tr.	The single section which was printed of the translation by Wood and Williams.

VOV	J. H. Newman, *Verses on Various Occasions.* This was originally published in London by Longmans, Green & Co in 1867. There have been numerous later editions.
MS(1)	Birmingham Oratory MS C7 8.
MS(2)	Birmingham Oratory MS C7 9. (These are the two notebooks containing Newman's handwritten translations intended for the Breviary translation project.)

Section 1 The Breviary translation

As noted in Chapter Four, Samuel Wood and Robert Williams undertook to publish an English translation of the Roman Breviary, using hymn translations made by Newman. The project began in 1838, was abandoned in November of that year, revived briefly in 1841, and abandoned again in the same year. Printing had been completed as far as page 192, finishing in the middle of a lesson at Matins for the fourth Sunday of Advent. This section appears to have been sewn up and made available to interested persons.

The translations which appear in this Section 1 are cited as they appear in the printed version. There are slight variations between this version, versions in Tract 75, and versions in *Verses on Various Occasions*.

The first twenty-eight hymns are from the Psalter. The Psalter of the Roman Breviary was completely revised, both in layout and in the allocation of the psalms over the days of the week, by Pius X in 1911. The text and allocation of the hymns were unchanged, however, and the Latin version from which Newman was translating (i.e. as 'corrected' by Urban VIII in 1632) can be consulted in any edition of the Roman Breviary. (The original version was retained in the Monastic Breviary and certain others, and may be consulted in the *Analecta Hymnica* as noted. The *Liturgia Horarum* has reverted to the original versions of the Latin hymns.)

1.

Sunday Matins (Winter) *Today the Blessed Three in One*
Primo die quo Trinitas (*Primo dierum omnium*)
Author unknown; sixth to seventh century AH 51:24
LH (Office of Readings, Sunday night, weeks 1 and 3) 3:550, 795; 4:498, 743.
Brev. Tr. p. 2 VOV p. 212 MS(1) 7 March 1837

2.

Sunday Matins (Summer) *Let us arise and watch by night*
Nocte surgentes vigilemus omnes
Author unknown; eighth to ninth century AH 51:26
LH (Office of Readings, Tuesday, weeks 2 and 4) 3:706, 953; 4:654, 901.
Brev. Tr. p. 3 Tract 75 p. 27 VOV p. 214

3.

Sunday Lauds (Winter) *Framer of the earth and sky*
Aeterne rerum conditor
St Ambrose AH 50:11
LH (Lauds Sunday, weeks 1 and 3) 3:554, 799; 4:502, 747
Brev. Tr. p. 20 VOV p. 226 MS(1) 21 March 1838

4.

Sunday Lauds (Summer) *Paler have grown the shades of night*
Ecce jam noctis tenuatur umbra
Author uncertain, perhaps Alcuin; eighth to ninth century AH 51:31
LH (Lauds Sunday weeks 2 and 4) 3:676, 923; 4:624, 871
Brev. Tr. p. 21 Tract 75 p. 52 VOV p. 229

5.

Prime *The star of morn to night succeeds*
Jam lucis orto sidere
Author unknown; at least eighth century AH 51:40
LH (Lauds Thursday weeks 2 and 4) 3:747, 992; 4:695, 940
Brev. Tr. pp. 22 and 29 Tract 75 p. 55

Newman did not include this translation in VOV, preferring the version in the Parisian Breviary (no. 46). The Marquess of Bute used it for his translation of the Breviary, stating that it had not previously been published. It had, however, been printed in Tract 75.

6.

Terce *Come, Holy Ghost, Who ever One*
Nunc Sancte nobis Spiritus
Author unknown. Very ancient. Has been attributed to St Ambrose, but this is doubtful AH 50:19
LH (Terce) 1:115, 316; 3:532; 4:480.
Brev. Tr. p. 37 Tract 75 p. 64 VOV p. 245
The version in VOV has been considerably amended.

7.

Sext *O God, the Lord of place and time*
Rector potens, verax Deus
Author uncertain. Very ancient. Has been ascribed to St Ambrose, but this is doubtful AH 50:20
LH (Sext) 1:116, 316; 3:533; 4:481
Brev. Tr. p. 40 Tract 75 p. 68 VOV p. 246
The first and third stanzas were considerably revised for the version in VOV, and the opening line is 'O God, Who canst not change nor fail'.

8.

None *O God, unchangeable and true*
Rerum Deus, tenax vigor
Author unknown. Very ancient. Has been ascribed to St Ambrose, but this is doubtful AH 50:20
LH (None) 1:116, 317; 3:534; 4:482
Brev. Tr. p. 44 Tract 75 p. 72 VOV p. 247

9.

Monday Matins *Sleep has refreshed our limbs, we spring*
Somno refectis artubus

Author unknown; sixth to seventh century AH 51:27
LH (Office of Readings, Monday night, weeks 1 and 3) 3:566, 812; 4:514, 760
Brev. Tr. p. 47 VOV p. 215 MS(1) 18 February 1838

10.

Monday Lauds *Of the Father Effluence bright*
Splendor Paternae gloriae
St Ambrose AH 50:11
LH (Lauds, Monday, weeks 1 and 3) 3:571, 816; 4:519, 764
Brev. Tr. p. 59 VOV p. 230 MS(1) 26 March 1838

11.

Tuesday Matins *O God from God, and Light from Light*
Consors Paterni luminis
Author unknown; sixth to seventh century AH 51:28
LH (Office of Readings, Tuesday night, weeks 1 and 3) 3:584, 830; 4:532, 778.
Brev. Tr. p. 61 VOV p. 217 MS(1) 23 February 1838

12.

Tuesday Lauds *Day's herald bird*
Ales diei nuntius
Prudentius, Cathemerinon 1 (*Ad galli cantus*): 1–8, 21–24, 81–84, 97–100 AH 50:23
LH (Office of Readings, Thursday night, weeks 2 and 4) 3:743, 988; 4:691, 936
Brev. Tr. p. 70 VOV p. 233 MS(1) 29 March 1838

13.

Wednesday Matins *Who madest all and dost control*
Rerum Creator optime
Author unknown; sixth to seventh century AH 51:28
LH (Office of Readings, Wednesday night, weeks 1 and 3) 3:602, 847; 4:550, 795
Brev. Tr. p. 71 VOV p. 218 MS(1) 8 March 1838

14.

Wednesday Lauds *Haunting gloom and flitting shades*
Nox et tenebrae et nubila
Prudentius, Cathemerinon II (*Hymnus Matutinus*): 1–8, 48, 49, 52, 57, 59, 60, 67, 68 AH 50:23
LH (Lauds, Wednesday, weeks 1 and 3) 3:606, 851; 4:554, 799 (different selection of lines)
Brev. Tr. p. 80 VOV p. 235 MS(1) 31 March 1838

15.

Thursday Matins *All tender lights, all hues divine*
Nox atra rerum contegit
Author unknown; sixth to seventh century AH 51:29
LH (Office of Readings, Thursday night, weeks 1 and 3) 3:619, 865; 4:567, 813
Brev. Tr. p. 81 VOV p. 220 MS(1) 14 March 1838

16.

Thursday Lauds *See, the golden dawn is glowing*
Lux ecce surgit aurea (*Sol ecce surgit igneus*)
Prudentius, Cathemerinon II: 25, 93, 94, 96–108 AH 50:24
LH (Lauds, Thursday, weeks 1 and 3) 3:622, 869; 4:570, 817 (different selection of lines)
Brev. Tr. p. 94 VOV p. 237 MS(1) 2 April 1838

17.

Friday Matins *May the dread Three in One, Who sways*
Tu Trinitatis Unitas
Author unknown; sixth to seventh century AH 51:29
LH (Office of Readings, Friday night, weeks 1 and 3) 3:637, 883; 4:585, 831
Brev. Tr. p. 94 VOV p. 222 MS(1) 15 March 1838

18.

Friday Lauds *Glory of the eternal Heaven*
Aeterna caeli gloria
Author unknown; seventh to eighth century AH51:32
LH (Lauds, Friday, weeks 1 and 3) 3:640, 887; 4:588, 835
Brev. Tr. p. 105 VOV p. 239 MS(1) 5 April 1838

19.

Saturday Matins *Father of mercies infinite*
Summae Parens clementiae (*Summae Deus clementiae*)
Author unknown; sixth to seventh century AH 51:30
LH (Office of Readings, Saturday night, weeks 1 and 3) 3:655, 901; 4:603, 849
Brev. Tr. p. 105 VOV p. 224 MS(1) 19 March 1838

20.

Saturday Lauds *The dawn is sprinkled o'er the sky*
Aurora jam spargit polum
Author unknown; seventh to eighth century AH 51:34
LH (Lauds, Saturday, weeks 1 and 3) 3:659, 906; 4:607, 854
Brev. Tr. p. 120 VOV p. 241 MS(1) 5 April 1838

21.

Sunday Vespers *Father of Lights, by Whom each day*
Lucis creator optime
Author unknown; sixth to seventh century. Attributed by some scholars to St Gregory the Great AH 51:34
LH (Second Vespers, Sunday, weeks 1 and 3) 3:562, 807; 4:510, 755
Brev. Tr. p. 123 Tract 75 p. 79 VOV p. 248

22.

Monday Vespers *Lord of unbounded space*
Immense caeli conditor
Author unknown; sixth to seventh century. Perhaps St Gregory AH 51:35
LH (Vespers, Monday, weeks 1 and 3) 3:580, 825; 4:528, 773
Brev. Tr. p. 125 VOV p. 250 MS(1) 10 April 1838

23.

Tuesday Vespers *All-bountiful Creator, who*
Telluris alme conditor (*Telluris ingeno conditor*)
Author unknown; sixth to seventh century. Perhaps St Gregory the Great AH 51:36

LH (Vespers, Tuesday, weeks 1 and 3) 3:597, 843; 4:545, 791
Brev. Tr. p. 128 VOV p. 252 MS(1) 10 April 1838

24.

Wednesday Vespers *O Lord, who, thron'd in the holy height*
Caeli Deus sanctissime
Author unknown; sixth to seventh century. Perhaps St Gregory the Great AH 51:36
LH (Vespers, Wednesday, weeks 1 and 3) 3:614, 860; 4:562, 808
Brev. Tr. p. 130 VOV p. 254 MS(1) 12 April 1838

25.

Thursday Vespers *O God, who hast given*
Magnae Deus potentiae
Author unknown; sixth to seventh century Perhaps St Gregory the Great AH 51:37
LH (Vespers, Thursday, weeks 1 and 3) 3:631, 878; 4:579, 826
Brev. Tr. p. 133 VOV p. 256 MS(1) 13 April (Good Friday) 1838

26.

Friday Vespers *Whom all obey*
Hominis superne Conditor (*Plasmator hominis, Deus*)
Author unknown; sixth to seventh century. Perhaps St Gregory the Great AH 51:38
LH (Vespers, Friday, weeks 1 and 3) 3:650, 896; 4:598, 844
Brev. Tr. p. 136 VOV p. 258 MS(1) 13 April 1838

27.

Saturday Vespers *The red sun is gone*
Jam sol recedit igneus (*O lux, beata Trinitas*)
Author unknown; seventh to eighth century AH 51:38
LH (Second Vespers, Sunday, weeks 2 and 4) 3:684, 931; 4:632, 879
Brev. Tr. p. 139 VOV p. 260 MS(1) p. 139, 1838 (*Sabbato Sancto*)

28.

Compline *Now that the day-light dies away*
Te lucis ante terminum
Author unknown; fifth to sixth century AH 51:42
Only the first stanza used in LH
Brev. Tr. p. 143 Tract 75 p. 84 VOV p. 261

29.

Advent Vespers *Maker of heaven, Eternal Light*
Creator Alme siderum (*Conditor alme siderum*)
Author unknown; at least ninth century AH 51:46
LH (Vespers, Advent) 1:113
Brev. Tr. p. 147, 162, 166, 174, 190 VOV p. 262 (first line: 'Creator of the starry pole') MS(2) 5 September 1838

30.

Advent Matins *Supernal Word, proceeding from*
Verbum supernum prodiens
Author unknown; at least tenth century AH 51:48
LH (Office of Readings, Advent) 1:114
Brev. Tr. p. 148, 162, 174, 190 VOV p. 264 MS(2) 7 September 1838

31.

Advent Lauds *Hark, a joyful voice is thrilling*
En clara vox redarguit (*Vox clara ecce intonat*)
Author unknown; at least tenth century AH 51:48
LH (Lauds, Advent) 1:114
Brev. Tr. p. 153, 166, 178 VOV p. 266 MS(2) 3 October 1838

Section 2 Translations in Tract 75

Newman provided translations of twelve office hymns in Tract 75; eight were used for the Breviary translation (included in Section 1). The remaining four hymns are given in this section.

32.

6 August – Transfiguration *O ye who seek the Lord*
Quicunque Christum quaeritis (Matins)
Prudentius, Cathemerinon XII, lines 1–4, 37–44, 85–88
Tract 75 p. 98 VOV p. 268

33.

6 August – Transfiguration *Light of the anxious heart*
Lux alma Jesu mentium (Lauds)
Author unknown. A cento from *Dulcis Jesu Memoria*, twelfth to thirteenth century
It is not known who composed the cento. It is a cento of lines not stanzas, and was much revised by Urban VIII. The original hymn was formerly ascribed to St Bernard.
Tract 75 p. 115 VOV p. 270

34.

10 August – St Laurence *Martyr of Christ, thy fight is won*
Invicte martyr unicum (Vespers) (*Martyr Dei qui unicum*) (from the Common of a martyr)
Author unknown; ninth century AH 51:129
LH (Common of a martyr) 1:1086; 2:1545; 3:1422; 4:1406
Tract 75 p. 119

35.

10 August – St Laurence *O God, of Thy soldiers*
Deus tuorum militum (Matins) (from the Common of a martyr)
Author unknown; fifth to seventh century AH 51:130
LH (Vespers, Common of a martyr) 1:1090; 2:1552; 3:1427; 4:1411
Tract 75 p. 121 VOV p. 272

Section 3 Manuscript translations for the Breviary translation

The translations in this section have not previously been published. (See Chapter Ten.)

36.

The Seven Sorrows of the Blessed Virgin *Cheerlessly and tearfully*
Stabat mater dolorosa
Author uncertain. Ascribed by some to Jacapone da Todi (d. 1306) AH 54:312
LH (Office of readings, Our Lady of Sorrows, 15 September) 4:1133
In the Roman Breviary in Newman's time, this feast was held on the Friday after Passion Sunday
MS(1) May 1838

37.

Vespers, Common of Apostles in Paschaltide *Deep in despair the Apostles were*
Tristes erant apostoli
Author unknown. Very ancient
LH (Vespers, Common of Apostles in Paschaltide) 2:1498
This hymn is the second part of the hymn *Aurora lucis rutilat* AH 51:89
MS(2) May 1838

38.

Christmas Vespers *Saviour of souls undone*
Jesu Redemptor omnium (*Christe, Redemptor omnium*)
Author unknown; sixth century AH 51:49
LH (Vespers, Christmas) 1:313, 318, 335
MS(2) 9 October 1838

39.

Christmas Lauds *From the rising of the day*
A solis ortus cardine
Sedulius AH 50:58
LH (Lauds, Christmas) 1:315
MS(2) 11 October 1838

40.

Holy Innocents – Matins *The jealous king is told*
Audit tyrannus anxius
Prudentius, Cathemerinon XII (*Hymnus Epiphaniae*): lines 93–100, 133–136 AH 50:27
LH (Lauds, Holy Innocents) 1:978 (including hymn 41)
MS(2) 12 October 1838

41.

Holy Innocents – Lauds and Vespers *Blossoms of the martyr band*
Salvete flores martyrum
Prudentius, Cathereminon XII (*Hymnus Epiphaniae*): lines 125–132
MS(2) 13 October 1838

42.

Epiphany Vespers *Why fear thy God should come*
Crudelis Herodes, Deum (*Hostis Herodes impie*)
Sedulius. Part of the hymn *A solis ortus cardine* AH 50:58
LH (Vespers, Epiphany) 1:440, 463
MS(2) 14 October 1838

43.

Epiphany Lauds *Greater far than cities great*
O sola magnarum urbium
Prudentius, Cathereminon XII (*Hymnus Epiphaniae*): 5–8, 61–64, 69–72, 77–80.
MS(2) 16 October 1838

44.

Lent – Sunday Vespers *Who hast the world's foundations cast*
Audi, benigne Conditor
Author unknown. Attributed by some to St Gregory the Great AH 51:53
LH (Vespers, Sunday, Lent) 2:29
MS(2) 17 October 1838

45.

Lent – Sunday Matins *Taught in the ancient mystic rite*
Ex more docti mystico
Author unknown. Attributed by some to St Gregory the Great AH 51:55
LH (Office of Readings, Sundays, Lent) 2:31
MS(2) 26 October 1838

Section 4 Translations of hymns in the Parisian Breviary

On the Parisian Breviary, cf. Chapter Three, note 20.

46.

Prime *Now that the day-stay glimmers bright*
Jam lucis orto sidere
Charles Coffin (1676–1749)
VOV p. 243
Newman translated this hymn at Littlemore in February 1842 at the request of Sir Francis Palgrave for the latter's *Anglo – Norman History.*

47.

Vespers – Common of a Confessor Bishop *O Thou, of shepherds Prince and Head*
Christe Pastorum caput atque princeps
The text in the Parisian Breviary is a version of a hymn from a breviary manuscript of the fifteenth century, author unknown, with considerable alterations by the compilers of the Parisian Breviary. The original version (AH 23:89) is now in use in LH (Office of Readings, Common of a Pastor) 1:1101; 2:1564; 3:1437: 4:1421.

Newman translated this hymn at Littlemore on 7 February 1842 at the request of Sir Francis Palgrave for the latter's *Anglo-Norman History*
VOV p. 274.

Appendices

APPENDIX ONE

Tracts for the Times *with a bearing on Liturgy*

Newman and other Tractarians published ninety Tracts over the years 1833–41 under the title *Tracts for the Times*. This was to have considerable influence in promoting a sense of the catholicity of the Church of England. Significant of the importance which the Tractarians attached to worship and sacraments, fifty-three of the Tracts have some bearing on liturgy. These are listed below according to author.

JOHN HENRY NEWMAN

1. Thoughts on the Ministerial Commission. (9 September 1833)
2. The Catholic Church. (9 September 1833)
3. Thoughts respectfully addressed to the Clergy on Alterations in the Liturgy. The Burial Service. The Principle of Unity. (9 September 1833)
6. The Present Obligation of Primitive Practice. A Sin of the Church (infrequent celebration of the Eucharist). (29 October 1833)
11. The Visible Church. (11 November 1833)
34. Rites and Customs of the Church. (1 May 1834)

38 and 41. *Via Media.* (25 July 1834, 24 August 1834)

75. On the Roman Breviary as embodying the substance of the devotional services of the Church Catholic. (24 June 1836)
76. Catena Patrum, No. 2, on baptismal regeneration. (29 September 1836)
78. Catena Patrum, No. 3. Testimony of Writers of the Later English Church to the Duty of maintaining, *Quod semper, quod ubique, quod ab omnibus traditum est.* (Usually attributed to H. E.

Manning and C. Marriott, but Newman may have been chiefly responsible for it.) (2 February 1837)

82. Letter to a Magazine on the Subject of Dr. Pusey's Tract on Baptism. (1 November 1837)

RICHARD HURRELL FROUDE

9. On Shortening the Church Service. Sunday Lessons. (31 October 1833)
63. The antiquity of the existing liturgies. (1 May 1835)

JOHN KEBLE

4. Adherence to the Apostolical Succession the Safest Course. On Alterations to the Prayer Book. (21 September 1833)
13. Sunday Lessons. The Principle of Selection. (5 December 1833)
52. Sermons for Saints' days and holidays. No. 1, St. Matthias (undated), 54. No. 2, The Annunciation (2 February 1835), 57. No. 3, St. Mark's day (25 March 1835), 60. St Philip and St. James (25 March 1835).

THOMAS KEBLE

84. Whether a clergyman of the Church of England be now bound to have Morning and Evening Prayers daily in his parish church. (24 August 1838). (Completed by George Prevost from p. 35.)

EDWARD BOUVERIE PUSEY

67. Scriptural views of holy baptism, pp. 1–48. (24 August 1835)
68. ditto, pp. 49–104. (29 September 1835)
69. ditto, pp. 105–208. (18 October 1835).
70. (In the 2nd edition of the Tracts, Tract 70 became the last part of tract on baptism pp. 209–295).
81. Catena Patrum, No. 4. Testimony of Writers in the Later English Church to the doctrine of the Eucharistic Sacrifice, with an historical account of the changes made in the Liturgy as to the expression of that doctrine. (1 November 1837)

ISAAC WILLIAMS

86. Indications of a superintending Providence in the preservation of the Prayer-book and in the changes which it has undergone. (25 March 1839)

ALFRED MENZIES

14. The Ember Days. (12 December 1833)

BENJAMIN HARRISON

16. Advent. (17 December 1833)
17. The Ministerial Commission: A Trust from Christ for the benefit of his people. (20 December 1833)

TEXTS AND REPRINTS

From the Anglican divines and other sources.

12. Richard Nelson, No. 1 (Bishops, Priests and Deacons). (4 December 1833). (T. Keble)
22. Richard Nelson, No. 2 (The Athanasian Creed). (6 January 1834). (T. Keble)
25. The Great Necessity and Advantage of Public Prayer. (25 January 1834). (Reprinted from Bishop Beveridge)
26. The Necessity and Advantage of Frequent Communion. (2 February 1834). (Reprinted from Bishop Beveridge)
27. The History of Popish Transubstantiation. (24 February 1834). (Reprinted from Bishop Cosin)
28. The same, concluded. (25 March 1834)
37. Bishop Wilson's form of Excommunication. (24 June 1834). (Reprinted from Bishop Thomas Wilson)
39. Bishop Wilson's form of receiving Penitents. (25 July 1834)
40. Richard Nelson, No. 3 (Baptism). (25 July 1834). (J. Keble)
42. Bishop Wilson's Meditations on his Sacred Office, No. 1. (24 August 1834)
43. Richard Nelson, No. 4 (Length of the Public Service). (21 September 1834). (T. Keble)
44. Bishop Wilson's Meditations on his Sacred Office, No. 2 (Monday). (29 September 1834)

46. Bishop Wilson's Meditations on his Sacred Office, No. 3 (Tuesday). (28 October 1834)
48. Bishop Wilson's Meditations on his Sacred Office, No. 4 (Wednesday). (30 November 1834)
50. Bishop Wilson's Meditations on his Sacred Office, No. 4 (Wednesday, continued). (26 December 1834)
53. Bishop Wilson's Meditations on his Sacred Office, No. 5 (Thursday). (24 February 1835)
55. Bishop Wilson's Meditations on his Sacred Office, No. 5 (continued). (25 March 1835)
56. Holy days observed in the English Church. (25 March 1835). (List compiled by J. W. Bowden)
62. Bishop Wilson's Meditations on his Sacred Office, No. 5 (continued). (1 May 1835)
64. Bishop Bull on the Ancient Liturgies. (11 June 1835)
65. Bishop Wilson's Meditations on his Sacred Office, No. 6 (Friday). (29 June 1835)
70. Bishop Wilson's Meditations on his Sacred Office, No. 7 (Saturday). (In later editions, this was incorporated into Tract 65.) (28 October 1835)
72. Archbishop Ussher on prayers for the dead. (6 January 1836)
88. The Greek Devotions of Bishop Andrewes. Translated and arranged by J. H. Newman. (25 March 1840)

APPENDIX TWO

Newman's Sermons of Liturgical Interest

The first column shows Newman's enumeration (he listed and numbered his Anglican sermons from 1 to 604).

In the second column, *P.S.* indicates that the sermon has been published in *Parochial and Plain Sermons*, and is followed by the volume number and number of the sermon in that volume. The remaining sermons are unpublished at present, and in this case the reference number of the sermon in the archives of the Birmingham Oratory is given.

The third column gives the date in the nineteenth century on which the sermon was delivered.

144	A.50.3 [1]	12.3.26	On Infant Baptism
152	A.17.1 [1]	30.7.26	On the Lord's Prayer
154	A.17.1 [1]	13.8.26	On the Ten Commandments (on sanctification)
156	A.50.3 [1]	10.9.26	On the Sacraments, etc.

167–172 A course of sermons on the two (dominical) sacraments

167	(not extant)		
168	*P.S.* VII, 16	15.6.28	Infant Baptism
169	A.50.3 [1]	22.6.28	On Infant Baptism (2)
170	B.3.6 [1]	29.6.28	Infant Baptism the doctrine of the Church (3)
171	A.17.1 [1]	6.7.28	On Confirmation
172	A.50.3 [1]	13.7.28	On the Lord's Supper

213	A.17.1 [1]	25.10.29	On the Duty of Public Worship

214	B.3.6 [1]	1.11.29	On Preaching

224–233 A course of sermons on the liturgy

224	A.50.3 [1]	31.1.30	The Liturgy the Service of the Priest (1)
225	A.50.3 [1]	7.2.30	The Liturgy Public – its three peculiar uses (2)
226	B.3.6 [II]	14.2.30	The Liturgy: *first*, teaches doctrine viz. concerning God (3)
227*	*P.S.* III, 6	21.2.30	Faith and Obedience
227*	A.6.14 [1]	21.2.30	The Liturgy: *first*, teaches doctrine
* listed thus			concerning man's duty (4)
228	B.3.6 [1]	28.2.30	The Liturgy: *first*, teaches doctrine concerning means of grace (5)
229	B.3.6 [1]	7.3.30	The Liturgy: *second*, forms the character, viz. to faith (6)
230	B.3.6 [1]	14.3.30	The Liturgy: *second*, forms the character, viz. to hope (7)
231	*P.S.* VII, 18	21.3.30	The Liturgy: *second*, forms the character, viz. to reverence: steadfastness in old paths (8)
232	B.3.6 [1]	28.3.30	The Liturgy forming the character: viz. to self-denial – the Commination and Lent Services (9)
233	B.3.6 [1]	4.4.30	The Liturgy forming the character: viz. to charity – the Litany (10)

280	*P.S.* II, 7	1.1.31	Ceremonies of the Church
287	*P.S.* VII, 2	27.2.31	Attendance on Holy Communion
290	A.50.5 [1]	20.3.31	On the objects and effects of preaching
348	A.50.3 [I] A.50.4 [II]	8.12.33	The Presence of Christ – various presences and in Holy Communion
358	*P.S.* III, 21	2.11.34	The Daily Service
360	A.17.1 [1]	16.11.34	Regeneration
381	A.50.3 [1]	23.11.34	Christian Sacraments contrasted to Jewish rites
363	*P.S.* II, 25	14.12.34	The Christian Ministry

387	*P.S.* III, 20	24.5.35	Infant Baptism
390	*P.S.* III, 18	8.11.35	The Gift of the Spirit
392	*P.S.* III, 19	15.11.35	Regenerating Baptism
449	A.50.5 [I]	19.3.37	The Institution of Holy Communion
459	A.50.3 [I]	23.4.37	On Holy Communion
496	*P.S.* IV, 23	15.4.38	Keeping Fast and Festival
505	*P.S.* VI, 11	13.5.38	The Eucharistic Presence
522	*P.S.* V, 1	2.12.38	Worship, a Preparation for Christ's coming

APPENDIX THREE

Newman's two prefaces to Hymni Ecclesiae

Newman wrote prefaces for the two anthologies entitled *Hymni Ecclesiae*, both of which were published in 1838 by J. H. Parker at Oxford.

The first preface was written in Latin. It is reproduced below, with an English translation following it. The other preface was written in English.

Preface to J. H. Newman's

Hymni Ecclesiae e Breviariis Romano, Sarisburiensi, Eboracensi et aliunde

Oxford: J. H. Parker 1838

Ne mirum tibi, Lector benevole, videatur, Hymnos, quos in manibus habes, et materie vetustos et stilo, hodiernis typis et hodiernorum favori esse commendatos. Non enim abs te exigitur, ut quicquid hic scriptum inveneris, id in sinum tuum recipias illico, absque animi ulla exercitatione aut judicio tuo. Neque qui totum aliquid edit in publicum, illum oportet universi operis in singula quaeque jurare, aut in rerum squalore immorari quod in antiquitate versatur. Alia nimirum sunt in monumentis veterum simplicis ac pristinae naturae elementa; prorsus aliud concretum vitium, et sordes temporum. Cordati autem hominis est, neque obsoleta pro priscis, nec peregrina pro falsis habere.

Quod quidem optimo consilio actum est olim a patribus nostris, qui, caeco quodam reformationis, quam vocant, aestu in Ecclesia passim fervente, e religionibus suis, non quae exterorum studium posceret, sed quae vis extorqueret, missa fecerunt; a malesana philosophia ereptis caeteris, ea concedendo, quae sanctitatem plane nullam, parem autem invidiam haberent. Hinc illi, quibus nunc utimur, ritus et caeremoniae; hinc rerum divinarum ordo; hinc et disciplinae nostrae forma et agendi ratio repetenda est.

Quod si fiat quaestio, cur diligentissimi viri, cum nostra omnia retractarent, hymnodiam solum intactam, et tanquam desperatam, ne dicam improbatam reliquerint, id vero ex ejusmodi silentio minime colligendum erit. Nam, cum statutum esset, ut cultus divinus, eo usque in Latino idiomate absolutus, transiret in vernaculam, quis daret, ut qui possent aliquid in rebus reformandis, ii in poetica florerent simul, verba autem in versum et quaestiones ad veritatis normam, pari solertia redigerent? Unde factum est, ut in officiis divinis, dum habemus caetera, hymnos non habeamus.

Quare in hac Ecclesiae nostrae qualicunque inopia, hoc tempore, Lector benevole, tibi apponenda statuimus illa vel illorum similia, quae nostri in saeculo decimo sexto, cum sua essent, de manibus prudenter amiserunt; non illa, ex omni parte approbanda, sed aspersa maculis, ita vero ut modo vix quicquam improbes, modo improbes, at neque ut rejicias nec tamen ut possis mederi. Nam quae tota reprobanda erant, ista scilicet tota omisimus; caetera subjicimus judicio tuo.

J.H.N.

(*Translation:* Let it not be a matter of wonder to you, gentle reader, that these hymns which you have before you, ancient both in content and style, have been printed in modern times and commended to the approval of people of the present age. For no demand is being made of you to take to heart at once whatever you find written here without reflecting on it and making an appraisal of it. Nor is there any obligation on an editor who publishes an entire work to justify each single item in the whole book or to dwell on the imperfections of style employed in ancient times. Undoubtedly there are other elements of a simple and primitive nature in the works of ancient authors: defects of a different sort developed and there was a meanness of style in those times. But it is the practice of a prudent man neither to consider that which is old to be out-of-date nor to hold what is strange to be spurious.

This indeed was the error committed with the best intention by our forefathers when they composed prayers amid the blinding fervour of what was called the Reformation, then raging throughout the Church. They composed new forms of prayer from their own convictions. The prayers were not based on what the study of other men's prayers would demand but what the strength of their enthusiasm compelled them to write. In the rest of their work they were moved by a disordered philosophy and admitted things which clearly lacked holiness and were equally a reproach. Hence those rites and ceremonies which we now use; hence our order of divine service; and from these sources must be traced both the form of our teaching and the principles of our worship.

If there is any question why these assiduous men left only the hymnody untouched, as if it were something to be despaired of, not to say disapproved of, even though they restructured all our forms of worship, at least this indeed can be deduced from a silence of this sort. For when it was decided that divine worship which had hitherto been entirely in Latin should be translated into the vernacular, who had any ability to offer in this area? Were there men able to do anything with the texts which were to be reformed who were at the same time flourishing poets and might with equal faculty render words into verse and relate their searchings to the norm of truth? So it came about that while we have everything else, we do not have hymns in our divine offices.

In view of this lack of office hymns in our Church, whatever its cause, we have decided to put before you, gentle reader, those hymns, or others like them, which our fathers in the sixteenth century considered it wise not to use. Those hymns are not worthy of approval in every respect: they are rough with blemishes, so that sometimes you will scarcely approve anything therein; sometimes you will approve, but while not rejecting them, you will not be able to improve them. For those hymns which must be accorded utter disapproval we have of course entirely omitted. The rest we submit to your judgment.)

The second preface, for the Parisian Breviary hymns, was written in English.

Preface to J. H. Newman's

Hymni Ecclesiae e Breviario Parisiensi

Oxford: J. H. Parker 1838

Of the three kinds of poetical composition, which, in accordance with the Apostle's direction, have ever been in use in the Church, 'Psalms and Hymns and Spiritual Songs', two are supplied by inspiration. We have no need, through God's bounty, to turn our thoughts to the composition of Psalms or Songs; and, to judge from the attempts which have been made, doubtless we are unequal to it. And the unapproachable excellence of the two which have been supplied serves to suggest the difficulties which beset the composition of the third which has not been supplied. Indeed, it is hardly too strong to say that to write Hymns is as much beyond us as to originate Psalmody. The peculiarity of the Psalms is their coming nearer than any other kind of devotion, to a converse with the powers of the unseen world. They are longer and freer than Prayers; and, as being so, are less a direct address to the Throne of Grace than a sort of intercourse, first with oneself, then with one's brethren, then with Saints and Angels, nay, even the world and all creatures. They consist mainly of the praises of God; and the very nature of praise involves a certain abstinence from intimate approaches to Him, and the introduction of other beings into our thoughts, through whom our offering may come round to Him. For as He, and He only, is the direct object of prayer, so it is more becoming not to regard Him as directly addressed in praise, which would imply passing a judgment on Him who is above all scrutiny and all standards. The Seraphim cried *one to another*, 'Holy, Holy, Holy', veiling their faces; neither looking nor speaking to Him. The Psalms, then, as being praises and thanksgivings, are the language, the ordinary converse, as it may be called, of Saints and Angels in heaven; and, being such, could not be written except by men who had heard the 'unspeakable things' which there are uttered. In this light they are more difficult than prayers. Beggars can express their wants to a prince; they cannot converse like his courtiers.

Much the same remark may be made about the Songs or Canticles of the Church, which are also inspired, and are a kind of Psalms written for particular occasions, chiefly occasions of thanksgiving. Such are the two Songs of Moses, the Song of Hannah, those in Isaiah, the Song of Hezekiah, of Habakkuk, of the Three Children, of Zacharias, of the Blessed Virgin, and of Simeon; most of which are in the Breviary, and the last four are retained in our own Reformed Prayer Book.

Yet though Hymns, as being of a measured length, and restrained metrically, are so far safer to attempt than Psalms or Songs, they have their own peculiar difficulties. They are direct addresses to Almighty God, which ever must be most difficult to the serious mind, whatever be the difficulty of other devotions. This, in the instance of Prayers, has led to the use of Sentences, such as occur in our own Services; which, besides the advantage of extreme brevity, for the most part admit of being taken from Scripture. It has led also to the repetition of the Lord's Prayer, and of the *Kyrie Eleison*; and again to the use of Collects, which lessen the difficulty of addressing God by subjecting it to fixed rules. Hence our best Family Prayers are what may be called a succession of Sentences strung together, the simple and concise expression of our humiliation, fear, hope, and desire, for ourselves and others. Long Public Prayers, to make a general assertion which of course admits of exceptions, are arrogant and irreverent; hence the Pharisees made them. Hence, too, the unchastised effusions which abound in the present day among those who have left the Church or lost her spirit. The great Eucharistic Prayer is nearly the only long prayer in the Catholic Church; and there is every reason to suppose that in its substance it proceeds from inspired authorities. In our own Service it has been separated by our Reformers into three distinct portions.

Hymns, however, being of the nature of praises, cannot be altogether brought down to that grave and severe character which, as being direct addresses to God, they seem to require; and this is their peculiar difficulty. To praise God specially for Redemption, to contemplate the mysteries of the Divine Nature, to enlarge upon the details of the Economy of Grace, and yet not to offend, to invoke with awe, to express affection with a pure heart, to be subdued and sober while we rejoice, and to make professions without display, and all this not under the veil of figurative language, as in the Psalms, but plainly, and (as it were) abruptly, surely requires to have had one's lips touched with a 'coal from the Altar', to have caught from heaven that 'new song' 'which no man could learn, but the hundred and forty and four thousand which were redeemed from the earth', the virgin followers of the Lamb.

Our Church, with the remarkable caution which she displays so often, has not attempted it. She has received the Psalms and Songs from Scripture; and, rejecting the Roman Hymns, has substituted in their stead, not others, but a metrical version of the Psalms. This abstinence has led on the one hand to some of her members on their own responsibility supplying the deficiency, and has incurred the complaint of others who argued that she ought to have taken on herself what, being right in itself, will certainly be done by private hands, if not by the fitting authority. But in truth, when it was necessary for her to abandon those she had received, nothing was left to her but to wait till she should receive others, as in the course of ages she had already received, by little and little.

The Roman Hymns, whether good or bad, were the work of no one generation, much less the outpourings of one mind. They were not the contents of one collection, published all new in a day according to the will of man. They were the gradual accumulation of centuries, bearing in old and new upon one treasure-house. When there was a call to reject them, there was nothing to be done but begin again. We could not be young and old at once. It was a stern necessity alone which could compel us to change from what we were; but being changed, so far we were not what we were, and must be what the primitive Church was in these respects, poor and ill-furnished. We began the world again. This is the proper answer to inconsiderate complaints and impatient interference. There have before now been divines who could write a Liturgy in thirty-six hours. Such is not our Church's way. She is not the empiric to make things to order, and to profess to anticipate the course of nature, which, under grace, as under Providence, is slow. She waits for that majestic course to perfect in its own good time, what she cannot extort from it; for the gradual drifting of precious things upon her shore, now one and now another, out of which she may complete her rosary and enrich her beads, beads and rosary more pure and true than those which at the command of duty she flung away.

As far as we know, the public Hymns of the early Church were not much more than the following: first, starting from Scripture, she adopted the repetition of *Hallelujah*, which is described by St. John, in the Revelations, to be the chant of the blessed inhabitants of heaven.

Next may be mentioned the *Gloria Patri*, pretty much as we now use it; thirdly, the *Trisagion*, or, 'Holy, Holy, Holy', from Isaiah vi.; or as it was also used, and now is, in the Roman Church, 'Sanctus Deus, Sanctus Fortis, Sanctus Immortalis'. Besides these, there was the Morning or Angelic Hymn, beginning with the words used by the Angels at the Nativity; and for the evening the Hymn beginning 'Hail gladdening Light', preserved by St. Basil. These are not metrical, as they were afterwards; nor are two others of a later date, which we still retain, the *Te Deum* and the *Athanasian Creed*. They are both of Gallican origin; though the former has been ascribed to St. Ambrose. Others, however, now extant, are certainly his; others are the compositions of St. Hilary, Prudentius, St. Gregory, and later saints. It is not too much to say then that, judging by what we know of the Hymns of the primitive Church, we should not be dissatisfied with the paucity of those which custom has, with a sort of tacit authority, introduced among us in the course of several centuries.

More, doubtless, might be selected from the writings of our sacred Poets; but since, from unhappy circumstances, such a work does not seem likely at the present day, thoughtful minds naturally revert to the discarded collections of the ante-reform era, discarded because of associations with which they were then viewed, and of the interpolations by which they were disfigured; but which, when purified from these, are far more profitable to the Christian than the light and wanton effusions which are their present substitute among us. Nay, even such as the Parisian, which are here first presented to the reader, which have no equal claims to antiquity, breathe an ancient spirit; and even where they are the work of one pen, are the joint and invisible contribution of many ancient minds. Moreoever, the ancient language used has a tendency to throw the reader out of every day thoughts and familiar associations, and to make him fervent without ceasing to be mortified. Many a man could bear to read the Canticles in a foreign language, who is unequal to it in his own.

It only remains to say, that the following selection of hymns, from the Paris Breviary, has been confined to such holy days and seasons as are recognized by our Church, or to special events or things recorded in Scripture; those Hymns, however, being omitted which contained invocations to the Saints of such a nature as to be, even in the largest judgment of charity, not mere apostrophes, but supplications.

21 February 1838. J.H.N.

Notes

The publication of *The Letters and Diaries of John Henry Newman*, in thirty-one volumes, was inaugurated by Charles Stephen Dessain with Volume XI in 1961. The volumes covering Newman's life in the Catholic Church have all been published, having been edited by Dessain (Volumes XVI–XXII) and by Dessain and Thomas Gornall (Volumes XXIII–XXXI). Since the death of Fr Dessain in 1976, six volumes covering Newman's life in the Church of England up to 1838 have been published, edited by Ian Ker and Thomas Gornall (Volumes I–IV), Thomas Gornall (Volume V) and Gerard Tracey (Volume VI).

(Volumes XVI–XXII were published by Thomas Nelson & Sons, Ltd, Walton-on-Thames; the remaining volumes by the Clarendon Press, Oxford.)

In the following notes, references to the above are given in the abbreviated form, *Letters and Diaries*, followed by volume number and page.

CHAPTER ONE *Beginnings*

1. Henry Tristram (ed.), *John Henry Newman: Autobiographical Writings* (London: Sheed & Ward, 1955), p. 49.
2. John Henry Newman, *Apologia pro vita sua* (London: Longmans, Green & Co., standard edition 1873), p. 18.

   Newman's indebtedness to Whately, Hawkins and others is recorded in Chapter 1 of the *Apologia*. His abandonment of Evangelicalism is treated in detail in Thomas L. Sheridan, *Newman on Justification* (New York: Alba House, 1967) especially Chapters 3 and 4.
3. A list of *Tracts for the Times* which have a bearing on liturgy, the sacraments and the services of the Church is given in Appendix One.
4. Newman came rather later to a study of the Caroline divines, and

certainly after his study of the Fathers. This probably took place as late as 1834 and perhaps, as Parker suggests, was due to the influence of Martin Routh, President of Magdalen. See Thomas M. Parker, 'The rediscovery of the Fathers in the seventeenth-century Anglican tradition', in John Coulson and A. M. Allchin (eds) *The Rediscovery of Newman: An Oxford Symposium* (London: Sheed & Ward and SPCK, 1967), pp. 31–49.

Among the many publications of works of the Caroline divines which accompanied the period of the Oxford Movement, Newman wrote prefaces for new editions of Sparrow's *Rationale of the Book of Common Prayer* (1839), Sutton's *Godley Meditations upon the most Holy Sacrament of the Lord's Supper* (1838) and *Disce Vivere* (1839), and Cosin's *A Collection of Private Devotions in the Practice of the Ancient Church called the Hours of Prayer* (1838). He translated and edited Andrewes's *Devotions (Preces Privatae)* (1842, originally Tract 88) and edited Wilson's *Sacra Privata* (1838). Newman also wrote prefaces to new editions of Edward Well's *Rich Man's Duty* (1840) and Nelson's *Life of George Bull* (1840). Keble edited an edition of Hooker's *Works* (1836). Faber was responsible for an edition of *The Private Devotions of Dr. William Laud* (1838).

CHAPTER TWO *Newman and the Liturgy*

1. G. J. Cuming, *A History of Anglican Liturgy* (London: Macmillan, 2nd edition, 1982), pp. 147–49.
2. J. Keble and J. H. Newman, *Remains of the late Reverend Richard Hurrell Froude, M.A., Fellow of Oriel College, Oxford* (London: J. G. & F. Rivington, 1838), Vol. I, p. 221.
3. Frederick Oakeley, *Historical Notes of the Tractarian Movement* (London: Longmans, Green & Co., with Roberts & Green, 1865), p. 13.
4. Cf. forthcoming article by the present author, 'John Henry Newman and the lectures of Professor Lloyd'.
5. Cuming, *A History of Anglican Liturgy*, p. 148.
6. William Palmer, *Origines Liturgicae, or Antiquities of the English Ritual and a Dissertation on Primitive Liturgies* (London: J. G. & F. Rivington, 4th edition, 1845), p. vi.
7. Froude's listing of the English order in the footnote (Tract 63,

p. 8; Keble and Newman, *Remains*, Vol II, p. 393) took no account of the fraction ordered by the rubrics during the Institution narrative. The version of the Tract printed in the *Remains* has an additional item, namely a synopsis in parallel columns of the consecration prayers of six primitive liturgies.

8. Keble and Newman, *Remains*, Vol I, p. 387. Letter to O (John Frederick Christie) from Barbados, 26 December 1834.
9. J. H. Newman, *A Letter to the Rev. Godfrey Faussett, M.A., Margaret Professor of Divinity, on certain points of faith and practice* (Oxford: J. H. Parker; London: J. G. & F. Rivington, 1838), p. 44f.
10. An account of the 'Bisley school' is given in Chapter Four. (See also Chapter Four, note 24.) As liturgical texts became available for study, some of the Tractarians began, like the non-Jurors, to prefer the 1549 Prayer Book to the 1552 and later versions: e.g. Newman in Tract 3 and Pusey in Tract 81. The short-lived 1549 Prayer Book was more 'Catholic' and more akin to the ancient liturgies. Newman suggested its use in order to drive the Evangelicals to support the 1662 Book instead of seeking to revise it. Pusey argued that the 1662 rite needed to be interpreted in the light of the 'genuine' English rite of 1549.
11. E. B. Pusey, *On the Tendency to Romanism Imputed to Doctrines Held of Old, as Now, in the English Church* (Oxford: 1839). Letter to the Bishop of Oxford.
12. At first Newman held, especially in Tracts 38 and 41 on the *via media*, that despite the influence of Bucer and other 'foreigners' on the English Reformers and on the Prayer Book itself, the latter had not been changed substantially in doctrine. Later, in Tract 71 on the Controversy with the Romanists, he qualified this view and admitted that the Reformers had introduced changes under the influence of Bucer and others.
13. This print is in the possession of Magdalen College.
14. 'The Parting of Friends', preached at the last anniversary of the foundation of the church at Littlemore which Newman attended, Monday, 25 September 1843. It was a service of Holy Communion celebrated by Pusey.
15. S. L. Ollard, *A Short History of the Oxford Movement* (London: Mowbray, 2nd edition, 1933). For a summary of some of the available evidence, pp. 154–72.
16. Ibid., p. 162. Also R. D. Middleton, *Newman and Bloxam: An*

Oxford Friendship (London: Oxford University Press, 1947), Chapter III; and *Magdalen Studies* (London: SPCK, 1936), pp. 34–41.

17. Ollard, *A Short History of the Oxford Movement*, p. 157 n. 5.
18. *Letters and Diaries*, XXI, 76–7. Letter 11 March 1864 to William John Fitzpatrick.
19. Newman does not seem to have possessed a copy of Palmer's *Origines Liturgicae.* His view of the Prayer Book owed more to the influence of writers such as Richard Mant, whose annotated edition of the Book of Common Prayer was published in 1820, and Joseph Bingham, who published his ten-volume work *Origines Ecclesiasticae* between 1708 and 1722. Newman presented a copy of the latter to John Bowden in 1835. *Letters and Diaries*, V, 24.

    See also Middleton, *Newman and Bloxam*, Chapter I. Middleton has recorded all the evidence about Newman at St Mary's Church.
20. Letter to his sister, Harriet (Mrs Thomas Mozley), 3 May 1837. Anne Mozley (ed.), *Letters and Correspondence of J. H. Newman during his life in the English Church* (London: Longmans, Green & Co., 1890), Vol. II, p. 231.

    See also *Letters and Diaries*, VI, 65.
21. Cf. letter Newman to Froude, 21 June 1834. Mozley, *Letters and Correspondence*, p. 50.

    See also *Letters and Diaries*, IV, 275. Newman's decision to have a daily celebration of the offices was partly influenced by Isaac Williams who had learnt the practice from Tom Keble at Bisley. See G. Prevost (ed.), *The Autobiography of Isaac Williams* (London: Longmans, Green & Co., 1892), pp. 75–6.
22. Middleton, *Newman and Bloxham*, pp. 8–11. Middleton has assembled the testimony of various persons to the effects of Newman's sermons.
23. Robert Wilberforce, *Doctrine of the Holy Eucharist* (Oxford: 1853). Tract 81 by Pusey and Benjamin Harrison, *Catena Patrum No. 4: Testimony of Writers of the Later English Church to the Doctrine of the Eucharistic Sacrifice, with an Historical Account of the Changes made in the Liturgy as the Expression of that Doctrine*, was published in November 1837. Like Newman, Pusey accepted the Real Presence, though not the doctrine of transubstantiation, and defended it throughout his life, especially in his sermons *The*

Holy Eucharist, a Comfort to the Penitent (1843; this was condemned by the University), *The Real Presence of Christ in the Holy Eucharist* (1853), *The Real Presence* (1857) and *Will ye also go away?* (1867).

Placid Murray, *Newman the Oratorian* (Dublin: Gill & Macmillan, 1969), pp. 43–58, deals with Newman's thought on the Eucharist, with special reference to his sermons. Tractarian thought on the Eucharist, with particular reference to Pusey and Keble, is dealt with by W. H. MacKean, *The Eucharistic Doctrine of the Oxford Movement* (London: Putnam, 1933). The most comprehensive and critical treatment of the subject is by Alf Härdelin, *The Tractarian Understanding of the Eucharist* (Uppsala: Acta Universitatis Upsalensis, 1965).

24. Murray, *Newman the Oratorian*, pp. 40–2, gives a list of 'seasonal' sermons.
25. Ibid., pp. 31–2.

CHAPTER THREE *Newman and the Breviary*

1. Prevost, *Autobiography of Isaac Williams* (3rd edition 1893), p. 37.
2. Frederick Oakeley, *Personal Reminiscences of the 'Oxford Movement'.* (Printed for the Islington Catholic Popular Club by Henry Teulon, 1855), p. 5.
3. Frederick Oakeley, *Reminiscences of Oxford by Oxford Men 1559–1850*, Lilian M. Quiller-Couch (ed.), (Oxford: Oxford Historical Society XXII and the Clarendon Press, 1892), pp. 324–8.
4. Prevost, *Autobiography of Isaac Williams*, p. 36.
5. Cologne, 25 August 1839. Quoted in John Edward Bowden, *The Life and Letters of Frederick William Faber.* (London: Burns & Oates, 1st edition, 1869), p. 65; and in Ronald Chapman, *Father Faber* (London: Burns & Oates, 1961), pp. 40–1.
6. Wilfrid Ward, *William George Ward and the Oxford Movement.* (London: Macmillan, 2nd edition, 1890), p. 93.
7. Ibid., p. 126.
8. H. P. Liddon, *Life of Edward Bouverie Pusey* (London: Longmans, Green & Co., 4 volumes, 1893–7), Vol II, p. 146.
9. Quoted in T. Mozley, *Reminiscensces, Chiefly of Oriel College and the Oxford Movement* (London: Longmans, Green & Co, 2nd edition, 1882), Vol I, p. 359.

10. Cf. Chapter Two, in note 4.
11. Keble and Newman, *Remains*, p. 365.
12. Newman, *Apologia*, p. 74.
13. Keble and Newman, *Remains*, pp. 402–3.
14. *Letters and Diaries*, V, 184. Mozley, *Letters and Correspondence*, Vol. II, p. 147. I have not been able to trace any discussion of the Breviary in the works of Nicholas Harpsfield (c.1519–75), Archdeacon of Canterbury in Mary's reign.
15. *Letters and Diaries*, V, 177.
16. Ibid., p. 176: diary entry Monday, 14 December.
17. *Letters and Diaries*, VI, 246.
18. Newman, *Apologia*, pp. 74–5.
19. *Letters and Diaries*, XXII, 4. Biographical details of Scott are given in XII, 430.
20. Taken from the hymn *Adeste, sanctae conjuges* from matins in the office of Holy Women in the Parisian Breviary of 1736. The hymn was written by Jean-Baptiste de Santeüil (1630–97), a Canon Regular of St Victor in Paris, who was one of the main hymn writers represented in the Parisian Breviaries of 1680 and 1736.

    The Parisian Breviary was the most notable of a number of reformed breviaries published by certain French, German and Austrian dioceses in the seventeenth and eighteenth centuries on their own authority. Dioceses such as Paris claimed Gallican privileges to set aside the Roman Breviary issued by Pius V in 1568 in favour of their own versions. The Parisian Breviary of 1736 was a radical reform. The psalms were rearranged, dominical and seasonal offices were secured from supersession by saints' feasts, the calendar was lightened, and other changes introduced. The new hymns in the Breviary, by authors such as Charles Coffin, Charles Guiet, Abbé Besnault, and the brothers de Santeüil, were of considerable interest and attracted the attention of some Anglicans who were interested in the office hymns. Newman presumably chose a verse from de Santeüil's hymn for the title page of Froude's *Remains* because he was at that time preparing a collection of these hymns, *Hymni Ecclesiae e Breviario Parisiensi*, a companion volume to his *Hymni Ecclesiae e Breviariis Romano, Sarisburiensi, Eboracensi et aliunde* (both published in 1838 by J.H. Parker). John Chandler, *Hymns of the Primitive Church* (London: John W. Palmer, 1837), included eighty hymns from the Parisian Breviary; his book consisted of Latin texts and his own verse translations. Like some of the Tractarians, he does not seem to have realised at that time how recent these hymns were. Isaac Williams published translations of many of these hymns in *The British Magazine* (see Prevost, *Autobiography of Isaac Williams*, p. 65), subsequently published in *Hymns Translated from the Parisian Breviary* (1839). He recorded in his *Autobiography* (pp. 36–7), 'At this time – about the year 1829 – I first became acquainted with the Parisian Breviary, with which I was very much struck, as was also John Keble, to whom I showed the book at Fairford, which was but a ride from Windrush. I was so taken with the hymns, that I translated several at that time with no idea of publication.' Williams added in a footnote printed in the 2nd and 3rd editions: 'December 6, 1859: . . . By-the-bye, when I was translating these breviary hymns for my personal edification at Windrush, there prevailed a general horror among Church people of unauthorised hymns being sung in church, and I remember I put them often into unrhythmical harsh metres to prevent this.' The illegitimate breviaries were gradually abandoned during the course of the nineteenth century in favour of the Roman Breviary, Paris being the last diocese to relinquish its breviary, in 1873.

21. *Letters and Diaries*, V, 246–7. Mozley, *Letters and Correspondence*, Vol. II, p. 177.
22. Keble and Newman, *Remains*, Vol. II, p. 379.
23. Quoted in Piers Brendon, *Hurrell Froude and the Oxford Movement* (London: Paul Elek, 1974), p. 141.
24. Cf. further discussion of Newman's sources for Tract 75 in Chapter Eight.
25. Isaac Williams wrote in his *Autobiography* (p. 114): 'And it was after this time that at Oakeley's suggestion, I understand, he used the prayers to the Virgin in the Breviary, which he had not done at first, and this is often the strong overt act towards joining that communion.'
26. *Letters and Diaries*, VI.
27. Ibid., pp. 46–8. Letter 25 March 1837 to Henry Wilberforce. The letter contains much interesting comment on the breviary offices.
28. Edwin A. Abbott, *The Anglican Career of Cardinal Newman* (London: Macmillan, 1892), Vol. I, p. 177.

CHAPTER FOUR *The Breviary Translation Project – Phase One*

1. *Letters and Diaries*, VI, 9. Mozley, *Letters and Correspondence*, Vol. II, pp. 221–2.
2. Letter to Newman, 13 August 1836. *Letters and Diaries*, V, 339. Mozley, *Letters and Correspondence*, Vol. II, p. 207.
3. Liddon, *Pusey*, Vol. II, pp. 152–3.
4. *Letters and Diaries*, VI, 192n.
5. Ibid.
6. Isaac Williams had been translating hymns from the Parisian Breviary for some years. His *Hymns Translated from the Parisian Breviary* was published in 1839.
7. Unpublished letter in Birmingham Oratory Archives.
8. Unpublished letter in Birmingham Oratory Archives.
9. Unpublished letter in Birmingham Oratory Archives dated 'Eve of St. Matthias' (23 February).
10. *Letters and Diaries*, VI, 218.
11. Unpublished letter Birmingham Oratory Archives.
12. Unpublished letter Birmingham Oratory Archives.
13. Unpublished letter Birmingham Oratory Archives.
14. *Letters and Diaries*, VI, 304–5.
15. Ibid., p. 312, n. 3.
16. Ibid., part quoted. Full text of letter in Birmingham Oratory Archives.
17. Ibid., pp. 327–41. For example, diary entries for 28 and 31 October and for 1 and 2 November.
18. All are unpublished letters in the Birmingham Oratory Archives.
19. This has not survived.
20. Quoted in Georgina Battiscombe, *John Keble: A Study in Limitations* (London: Constable, 1963), p. 199.
21. At St Mary's 1831–36 and at Littlemore until 1837.
22. Cf. Chapter Three, note 20.
23. He was curate to Tom Keble at Bisley 1842–48; then, because of failing health, he moved to Stinchcombe where he assisted George Prevost, his brother-in-law.
24. The other members of the 'Bisley school' were Hubert Cornish, Charles Cornish, Robert Gregory, H. A. J. Jeffreys, Raymond Barker, Errol Hill, and Richard Champernowne. O. W. Jones, *Isaac Williams and his Circle* (London: SPCK, 1971).
25. He changed his views later in life and became critical of Newman

and the Tractarians. He edited Isaac Williams's *Autobiography*. The possibility cannot be ruled out that his editing was coloured by bias against the movement.

26. Letter from Elizabeth Keble to John, dated simply 'Friday morning', presumably written fairly soon after June 1836. Keble College Archives, Keble Family Letters, Folio 26. Many of the Keble family letters were undated or headed only with the day of the week. Another letter in Folio 26 (which contains 102 letters from Elizabeth to John 1806–1842) is a very short one dated simply 'Monday morning' and containing in the middle of the usual family chat the inexplicable sentence 'I am very glad to hear of their Breviary which I had not before.'
27. Next five words illegible.
28. Probably to lend weight to her words, she addressed him here by the family nickname 'Charles'.
29. Part 2 (i.e. volumes 3 and 4) of Froude's *Remains* were published in the following year, 1839. It was hoped that the contents of the two volumes in part two would redress the disapproval aroused by vols. 1 and 2 (published 1838), and Keble wrote a special preface for volume 3.
30. *Tract 81: Catena Patrum, No. 4. Testimony of Writers in the later English Church to the doctrine of the Eucharistic Sacrifice, with an historical account of the changes made in the Liturgy as to the expression of that doctrine.* Published 1 November 1837.
31. Letter from Elizabeth Keble to John dated 'October 30th, Thursday' in Keble College Archives, Keble Family Letters Folio 27. Georgina Battiscombe, who quoted a few lines of this letter (*John Keble*, p. 200), wrongly assigns this letter to 1836 as 30 October did not fall on a Thursday in 1836, but it did in 1838. More importantly the other correspondence quoted in the present chapter indicates beyond doubt that the actual initiation of the translation project took place in 1838. Battiscombe also assigns too much of this initiative to Newman personally, overlooking the part played by Wood and Williams.
32. Keble College Archives, Keble Family Letters Folio 14. A note to Elizabeth written at the end of a letter to Tom Keble. Battiscombe (p. 200) wrote: 'His reply is dated November 14th 1836'. In fact this letter is dated simply 'Nov. 14'. Elsewhere in a different hand (presumably that of an archivist) has been written '1836 Qu(ery)'.

    For the reasons given in the previous footnote this letter must have been written in 1838. Presumably Battiscombe, who does not cite references for these two letters in her footnotes, has been misled by the suggested date of 1836, especially as this is the year in which Tract 75 was published.

Jones, *Isaac Williams and his Circle*, p. 43, also wrongly assigns the actual beginning of the translation project to 1836, and like Battiscombe overlooks the initiative taken by Wood and Williams.

33. *Letters and Diaries*, VI.
34. Ibid.
35. Ibid., pp. 336–7. Keble tried to moderate Prevost's attacks on Newman by suggesting that Newman was not responsible for the Breviary translation project. To this Prevost retorted: 'Formally perhaps he is not, but virtually he is so, for, had he felt as he ought, I do not think these young men would have taken such a thing into their heads.' Jones, *Isaac Williams and his Circle*, p. 45.
36. *Letters and Diaries*, VI, 338, n. 1.
37. Ibid., p. 338. The Roman Catholic Church in England did not adopt the Sarum Breviary, despite this suggestion. When Westminster Cathedral was opened in 1903, it was suggested that the Sarum Breviary should be used for the liturgical hours, but this idea was not taken up.
38. Ibid., pp. 338–9. Mozley, *Letters and Correspondence*, Vol. II, pp. 266–7.
39. *Letters and Diaries*, VI, 339.
40. Ibid.
41. Ibid., p. 340.
42. Ibid., p. 341.
43. That is, the Festa Sanctorum. Saints' feasts presented more problems than the Proper of Time: firstly, whether to omit all saints feasts which were not in the calendar of the Book of Common Prayer; secondly, whether to retain some not in the Prayer Book Calendar, such as St Thomas of Canterbury; thirdly, what to omit from the hagiographical lessons at Matins.
44. Unpublished letter in Birmingham Oratory Archives. The footnote suggests that Newman must have offered to pay for the extra cost of altering what had been set up in print, either with the assistance of others, or by himself.
45. *Letters and Diaries*, VI, 343.
46. Unpublished letter in Birmingham Oratory Archives.
47. Wood was more 'High Church' than Williams, who within a few

years was to move over to Evangelicalism. It is likely that his earlier attachment to High Church principles was due to the persuasion of Wood.

48. Unpublished letter in Birmingham Oratory Archives. There is also a lengthy footnote, not printed here, containing various notes about possible approaches to correcting the objectionable elements in the Breviary.
49. Birmingham Oratory Archives. Most of this letter is quoted in *Letters and Diaries*, VI, 343, n. 2.
50. *Letters and Diaries*, VI, 342.
51. Ibid., p. 345.
52. Ibid., pp. 345–7. Mozley, *Letters and Correspondence*, Vol. II, pp. 267–9.
53. *Letters and Diaries*, VI, 348, 356.
54. Ibid., cf. p. 355n. Mozley, *Letters and Correspondence*,Vol. II, pp. 270–1.
55. Prevost, *Autobiography of Isaac Williams*, pp. 103–4.
56. *Letters and Diaries*, VI, 344.

CHAPTER FIVE *The Breviary Translation Project – Phases Two and Three*

1. Unpublished letter in Birmingham Oratory Archives.
2. Magdalen College, Oxford, Bloxam MS section 304, p. 300. Letter is dated 'Infra Oct. Apost. 1841'.
3. Ibid., p. 301. Letter is dated 'In fer. 4 post Dom. infra Oct. Asc.'
4. Charles Seager, a learned orientalist, spent four years as Pusey's assistant before becoming a Catholic. He did not complete his publication of the Latin text of the Sarum Breviary. Two parts were, however, published in 1842 and 1855. (See following chapter.)
5. Magdalen College Bloxam MS section 304, pp. 302–3. 'Leslie' is the publisher J. Leslie of 52 Great Queen Street, Lincoln's Inn Fields, London.
6. E. A. Knox in *The Tractarian Movement 1833–1845* (London: Putnam, 1933), pp. 192–6, writing from an Evangelical stance, and hostile to Newman and the Oxford Movement, gives a good account of how uncongenial the use of the Roman Breviary would be to a convinced Protestant.

7. Magdalen College Bloxam MS section 304, pp. 300.
8. Mozley, *Letters and Correspondence*, Vol. II, p. 347.
9. Unpublished letter in Birmingham Oratory Archives, folio 104, p. 55.
10. Magdalen College Bloxam MS section 304, p. 304.
11. Cf notes 16 and 31 below.
12. Magdalen College Bloxam MS section 304, p. 302.
13. *Apologia*, p. 74.
14. Unpublished letter in Birmingham Oratory Archives.
15. Cf. Liddon, *Pusey*, Vol. II, pp. 388–90.
16. Anon (Maria Trench), *The Story of Dr. Pusey's Life* (London: Longmans, Green & Co., 1900), p. 229.
17. Quoted in Jones, *Isaac Williams and his Circle*, p. 86. This letter and the remainder of the information given by Jones on pp. 86 and 87 refers not to the Sarum Breviary project, as the author claims, but to the third phase of the Roman Breviary translation project.

    Another misleading account of the second phase of the project is given in Middleton's *Newman and Bloxam* pp. 93–5. This account is based on the material in the Magdalen College Bloxam MS. Middleton dated the project from 1841, evidently unaware of the first phase of the project in 1838 or of the involvement of Samuel Wood. In addition he confused the Roman and Parisian Breviaries (on p. 94, n. 1): he quoted (from Prevost, *Autobiography of Isaac Williams*) to show that Isaac Williams had become acquainted with the Roman Breviary in 1829, but this referred to the Parisian Breviary; the full quotation is reprinted in Chapter Three, note 20.
18. Jones, *Isaac Williams and his Circle*, pp. 86–7.
19. Liddon, *Pusey*, Vol. II, p. 396.
20. Ibid. Quoted p. 390. The date of this letter is 2 December not 2 October.
21. Ibid., p. 390.
22. Unpublished letter in Birmingham Oratory Archives, from Pusey to Newman. Undated, presumably written between Newman's letters of 2 December and 18 December.
23. Quoted in Liddon, *Pusey*, Vol. II, p. 391; original in Birmingham Oratory Archives.
24. Liddon, *Pusey*, Vol. II, p. 392.
25. Ibid., pp. 392–3.

26. Quoted in Trench, *Pusey's Life*, pp. 230–1.
27. Unpublished letter in Keble Family Letters, Keble College Archives, Folio 15.
28. Trench, *Pusey's Life*, p. 231.
29. Unpublished letter in Birmingham Oratory Archives.
30. Birmingham Oratory (ed.), *Correspondence of John Henry Newman with John Keble and others 1839–1845* (London: Longmans, Green & Co. 1917), p. 306.
31. Ibid., pp. 307–8
32. Unpublished letter in Birmingham Oratory Archives.
33. Liddon, *Pusey*, Vol. II, p. 396.
34. Cf. letter from Robert Williams to Bloxam 4 June 1841. Magdalen College Bloxam MS section 304, pp. 302–3.
35. A copy is held in the Birmingham Oratory Archives, ref. A 162. Inquiries have so far revealed the existence of only one other extant copy. This printed part of the translation is referred to by Bloxam in the note in Magdalen College Bloxam MS section 304, p. 300, quoted above. According to Oakeley's letter to Pusey (quoted above, cf. note 16) 20 November 1843, the whole of the translation had been completed in manuscript except the hymns: these manuscripts have not survived.
36. Anglican office books were produced at least as early as the seventeenth century, e.g. Cosin's *Private Devotions in the Practice of the Ancient Church, called the Hours of Prayer* (1627) and Austin's *Devotions in the Ancient Way of Offices* (1683). Later office books include Dorrington's *Reformed Devotions disposed into the form and method of the Roman Breviary* (1719), Hele's *Select Offices of Private Devotion* (1832), and Acland-Troyte's *The Hours* (1841). Many more Anglican office books have been published since, mostly consisting of selections from the Roman or Sarum or Monastic Breviary, and often adapted to the needs of Anglican Religious Communities.

    Peter F. Anson, *The Call of the Cloister* (London: SPCK, revised edition 1964), gives a long list of such publications ranging in date from 1627 to 1955. The first Anglican translations of the whole breviary were probably (a) the English version of the Sarum Breviary compiled by the Society of the Most Holy Trinity 1889 (see next chapter) and (b) the English translation of the Roman Breviary in *The Divine Office*. This latter Anson (pp. 613–17) lists as published in 1953 by the Society of St Margaret, East Grinstead.

The first Roman Catholic translation of the Roman Breviary was that of the Marquess of Bute, 1879. There have subsequently been other Roman Catholic translations, notably those produced by the Nuns of Stanbrook Abbey (Burns Oates & Washbourne, 1936) and by the Liturgical Press, Collegeville (Latin text and English translation), 1964.

CHAPTER SIX *The Sarum Breviary Project*

1. Liddon, *Pusey*, Vol. II, p. 146.
2. The ancient psalter of the Roman Breviary remained unchanged until the new psalter of 1911 was issued.
3. These two schemes have been tentatively dated 1538 and 1540–41. The texts have been edited by J. W. Legg in *Cranmer's Liturgical Projects* (Henry Bradshaw Society 1915). Cf. also F. A. Gasquet and E. Bishop *Edward VI and the Book of Common Prayer* (London: John Hodges, 1890), Chapters II and III, and Appendices II and III. These appendices are not given in the later editions of this work published by Burns & Oates.
4. Quoted in Liddon, *Pusey*, Vol. II, pp. 146–7.
5. Ibid., p. 147.
6. Cf. Härdelin, *The Tractarian Understanding of the Eucharist*, pp. 53–4.
7. Liddon, *Pusey*, Vol. II, p. 147.
8. Ibid., p. 148.
9. Magdalen College Bloxam MS section 304, p. 303.
10. R. W. Church, *The Oxford Movement*, Geoffrey Best (ed.), (Chicago: University of Chicago Press, 1970), p. 162.
11. *Letters and Diaries*, XII, 245.
12. Ibid., p. 245, n. 3.
13. Two editions of the first section were issued:

    1. *Ecclesiae Anglicanae Officia Antiqua Portiforii seu Breviarii Sarisburiensis … Fasciculus Primus*, printed by C. J. de Mat et Soc., Brussels, and published in 1842 by J. Leslie, 52 Great Queen Street, Lincolns Inn, London.

    2. As 1 but published in 1843 by J. Leslie. The second section was published with a slightly different title and by a different publisher: *Breviarii Sarisburiensis fasciculus secundus* … printed by the Margareta Leistenschneider Press at Trèves, and published in 1855 by Whittaker, Ave Maria Lane, London.

14. Cf. F. Procter and W. H. Frere, *A New History of the Book of Common Prayer* (London: Macmillan, 1905), p. 350, n. 3.
15. F. Procter and C. Wordsworth (eds), *Breviarum ad Usum Insignis Ecclesiae Sarum* (London: Cambridge University Press, 3 vols, 1879–86). Cf. also W. H. Frere, *The Use of Sarum* (London: Cambridge University Press, 2 vols, 1898, 1901).
16. Cf. Anson, *The Call of the Cloister*, pp. 613–17.
17. *The Breviary of the Renowned Church of Salisbury. Rendered into English according to the use of the Society of the Holy Trinity, Devonport* (London: Gilbert and Rivington, 1889). Translated and edited by Sister Amelia Warren. Cf. Anson, *The Call of the Cloister*, pp. 273, 616.

CHAPTER SEVEN *The Breviary Offices at Littlemore*

1. Letters from Newman to Henry Wilberforce 25 March and 9 May 1837. *Letters and Diaries*, VI, 46–9, 65–7. The former letter is quoted in Chapter Three above.
2. E. Hermitage Day (ed.), 'Letters from Oxford and Littlemore: An unpublished correspondence on the Oxford Movement', in *The Treasury* (1911), pp. 22–6, 119–24.

   Extracts from two letters written by Dalgairns, together with much interesting information about Littlemore, are given in Fr Bernard Basset's booklet, *Newman at Littlemore*, published in 1983 by the Friends of Cardinal Newman at Birmingham Oratory.
3. Newman, *Apologia*, pp. 173–6. Full text in Mozley, *Letters and Correspondence*, Vol. II, pp. 392–4.
4. Newman, *Apologia*, pp. 176–7.
5. Letter to Copeland, 10 March 1846, after he had removed his belongings from Littlemore in February 1846. *Letters and Diaries*, XI, 132–3.
6. William Lockhart, 'Cardinal Newman: Or 'Tis Fifty Years Since', *Dublin Review* (October 1890) p. 422. Lockhart wrote a description containing similar details in reply to Bloxam's request for reminiscences in the 1880s: Magdalen College Bloxam MS section 304, p. 456.
7. Oakeley, *Personal Reminiscences of the 'Oxford Movement'*, p. 17.
8. Magdalen College Bloxam MS section 304, pp. 456 (Lockhart), 545–6 and 547 (Stanton), 546 (Christie).

9. Birmingham Oratory Archives. Quoted in Henry Tristam, 'Littlemore' in *Newman and Littlemore: A Centenary Anthology and Appeal* (Littlemore, Oxford: The Salesian Fathers, 1945), p. 17.
10. Mark Pattison, *Memoirs* (London: Macmillan, 1888), p. 189.
11. Ibid., pp. 190, 193.
12. It would seem, from Stanton's reminiscences quoted below, that the Calendar of the Book of Common Prayer was followed in the recitation of the Roman Breviary at Littlemore.
13. Dalgairns wrote the lives of several saints associated with the Cistercian order for Newman's series 'Lives of the English Saints' (1844 seq.): St Stephen Harding, founder of the order; St Aelred, abbot of Rievaulx; and St Gilbert of Sempringham, who founded an order based on the Cistercian model.
14. Richard Stanton, 'Some Reminiscences of the Early Days of Cardinal Newman's Catholic Life', *Dublin Review* (October 1890), pp. 403–4.
15. Actually there was by no means any uniform pronunciation of Latin among Roman Catholic priests at this time. Most priests tended to pronounce Latin like their own vernacular, and at the First Vatican Council the reporters had to be specially trained to record the speeches of bishops with French, Spanish, German and other national pronunciations. Some of the Council Fathers found difficulty in following each other's Latin speeches. However, the spread of the Italianate pronunciation was one of the by-products of the First Vatican Council as the power of the papacy increased and became more centralised. Another factor in the spread of this pronunciation was the restoration of Gregorian chant, for which Pius X commended the Italianate pronunciation as being the most suitable for singing.

    In Newman's time, the English pronunciation of Latin differed considerably from the various Continental pronunciations. Since the time of Erasmus, the pronunciation of Latin in England had followed the changes in English phonetics closely. This was true of both Anglican and Roman Catholic practice. Roman Catholic priests used the Anglicised pronunciation but gave the vowels just enough of a Continental sound to preserve the rhymes. The Littlemore community were aware that Church Latin was pronounced differently on the Continent, but saw no incongruity in using the Anglicised or 'Oxford' pronunciation.

    Nevertheless, the Oxford Movement was to play a large part in the adoption by English Roman Catholic clergy and choirs of the Italian pronunciation during the second half of the nineteenth century. This was due to the preference of many of the converts for the Italian pronunciation. There was inevitably some resistance from non-convert priests to what they saw as a new-fangled pronunciation consisting of 'chees' and 'chaws', but eventually the Italian pronunciation prevailed.

The 'Oxford' pronunciation used by Newman and his companions at Littlemore is not, of course, to be confused with what is now known as the Oxford (or the reformed classical) pronunciation, namely the attempted reconstruction of literary Latin as used by educated Romans in the age of Cicero. This was adopted in the 1870s and is now widely used in schools and universities.

See also F. Brittain, *Latin in Church* (Cambridge: Cambridge University Press, 1934).

16. Newman later became devoted to the Italianate pronunciation, especially after study and novitiate in Rome. On 7 August 1849 he wrote to Faber: 'What with new priests and old priests, we have such varieties in saying Mass, that I propose bringing it before the Deputies – "that in saying Mass the Italian pronunciation of Latin is the Rule of the English Oratory" ...' *Letters and Diaries*, XIII, 331.
17. Oakeley, *Historical Notes of the Tractarian Movement*, pp. 98–9.

    Father Dominic arrived at Littlemore on the evening of 8 October. He did not 'ask his way to Mr Newman's'. Dalgairns met his coach, greatly delayed, at Oxford, and brought him to Littlemore in a chaise, arriving at about eleven.

CHAPTER EIGHT *Newman's Writings on the Daily Office*

1. Cf. Chapter Three, especially p. 23 and notes 22, 23, 24.
2. Cf. Chapter Four, especially note 1.
3. Cf. Chapter Three for details.
4. Cf. correspondence cited in Chapter Five.
5. However, some Anglicans were purchasing copies from Booker, a Roman Catholic bookseller in London, as early as the late-1820s and, at a later date, from William Parker in Oxford. Cf. Chapter Three.
6. Cf. Anson, *The Call of the Cloister*, pp. 613–17.

7. Cf. W. Jardine Grisbrooke, 'A Contemporary Liturgical Problem: The Divine Office and Public Worship', *Studia Liturgica*, 8:3 (1971–2), 9:1–3 (1973). Also W. Jardine Grisbrooke, 'The Divine Office: The Formative Period – Cathedral and Monastic Offices' and J. D. Crichton, 'The Divine Office: The Office in the West: The Early Middle Ages' both in Cheslyn Jones, Geoffrey Wainwright and Edward Yarnold (eds), *The Study of Liturgy*, (London: SPCK, 1978), pp. 358–77.
8. Cf. forthcoming work by the present author 'The Office Hymn in the West'.
9. All written by Dom Anselmo Lentini, OSB, who headed the group responsible for the Latin hymns in the *Liturgia Horarum*. (Cf. note 8 above.)
10. Cf. Anson, *The Call of the Cloister*, pp. 613–17.
11. Bute stated in a footnote that the hymn had not been published. In fact it had been published in Tract 75, though not included by Newman in *Verses on Various Occasions*.
12. Birmingham Oratory archives C7 9 (containing the Psalter hymns) and C7 8 (containing the remaining hymns).
13. This sermon is no. 358 in Newman's own enumeration of his 604 Anglican sermons and was published in *Parochial and Plain Sermons*, Vol. III, Sermon 21.
14. Mozley, *Letters and Correspondence*, Vol. II, p. 50. *Letters and Diaries*, IV, 275–6. Although this section was written on 21 June, Newman had begun the letter on 14 June.
15. Mozley, *Letters and Correspondence*, Vol. II, pp. 51–2. *Letters and Diaries*, IV, 290. R. F. Wilson, of Oriel, curate of Bocking, Essex, corresponded from time to time with Newman. Cf. *Letters and Diaries*, IV, 328.
16. Tract 84, published 24 August 1838: 'Whether a clergyman of the Church of England be now bound to have Morning and Evening Prayers daily in his parish church.' The Tract was completed from p. 35 by George Prevost.
17. Prevost, *Autobiography of Isaac Williams*, pp. 75–6.
18. Ibid., p. 75.

CHAPTER NINE *Outcome: 'This is a religion'*

1. Newman, *Apologia*, p. 176.
2. Ibid., p. 165.

3. Ibid.
4. In September 1844 Newman gave Holy Communion to his friend John Bowden just before he died.
5. Birmingham Oratory, *Correspondence of Newman with Keble*, pp. 351 and 364.
6. The Tractarians were very interested in the notes of the Church, and William Palmer discussed them at great length in his two-volume work *Treatise on the Church of Christ* (1833).
7. J. H. Newman, *Essays Critical and Historical*, (London: Longmans, Green & Co., 5th edition, 1885), Vol. II, pp. 11–12.
8. Ibid., p. 47.
9. Newman, *Apologia*, p. 139.
10. *Correspondence of Newman with Keble*, p. 218.
11. Second Vatican Council, *Constitution on the Sacred Liturgy* (*Sacrosanctum Concilium*), 2.
12. Newman, *Apologia*, p. 166.
13. Ibid., p. 340.

CHAPTER TEN *Ten Translations*

1. See Chapter Eleven, Section 3. Cf. also pp. 28, 97–9.

CHAPTER ELEVEN *Notes on the Translations*

1. G. M. Dreves, C. Blume, and H. M. Bannister (eds), *Analecta Hymnica Medii Aevi*. Published in fifty-five volumes at Leipzig between 1886 and 1922 by O. R. Reisland.

   An index to this work was published by Francke in 1978. Max Lutolf (ed.), *Analecta Hymnica Medii Aevi: Register I* (two volumes) and *Register II* (one volume), (Bern and Munich: Francke, 1978).
2. A useful reference work concerning the hymns of the Roman Breviary is Joseph Connelly, *Hymns of the Roman Breviary* (London: Longmans, Green & Co., 1957).

   For the hymns of the *Liturgia Horarum*, Anselmo Lentini (ed.) *Te decet hymnus: L'Innario della 'Liturgia Horarum'* (Vatican: Typis Polyglottis Vaticanis, 1984).

Select Bibliography

(Biographies and standard works on the Oxford Movement have not been included unless specifically referred to in this book.)

UNPUBLISHED SOURCES

Birmingham Oratory Archives

Unpublished sermons by Newman (see Appendix Two, p. 143).
Index of Newman's Anglican Sermons.
C 7 8, C 7 9: manuscript notebooks containing hymn translations by Newman.
Notes made by Newman in the Bodleian 2 May 1836 in preparation for Tract 75.
A 162: fascicule of Breviary translation by Williams and Wood.
Unpublished letters to and from Newman (references in notes to Chapters Four and Five).

Keble College, Oxford, Archives

Keble Family Letters, especially folios 14, 15, 26, 27.

Magdalen College, Oxford, Archives

Bloxham MSS, especially section 304 (references in Chapters Five, Six and Seven).

PUBLISHED SOURCES

Baker, William J., *Beyond Port and Prejudice: Charles Lloyd of Oxford 1784–1829.* Orono: University of Maine at Orono Press, 1981.
Barmann, Lawrence F., 'The Liturgical Dimension of the Oxford

Tracts 1833–1841'. *The Journal of British Studies* (Trinity College, Hartford, Connecticut) 7:22 (May 1986), pp. 92–113.

Basset, Bernard, *Newman at Littlemore*. Birmingham Oratory: The Friends of Cardinal Newman, 1983.

Battiscombe, Georgina, *John Keble: A Study in Limitations*. London: Constable, 1963.

Brendon, Piers, *Hurrell Froude and the Oxford Movement*. London: Paul Elek, 1974.

Brilioth, Ynge, *The Anglican Revival: Studies in the Oxford Movement*. London: Longmans Green, 1925.

Brittain, F., *Latin in Church*. Cambridge: CUP, 1934.

Chapman, Ronald, *Father Faber*. London: Burns and Oates, 1961.

Connelly, Joseph, *Hymns of the Roman Breviary*. London: Longmans Green, 1957.

Coulson, John *and* Allchin, A. M. (eds), *The Rediscovery of Newman: An Oxford Symposium*. London: Sheed & Ward/SPCK, 1967.

Courtney, W. P. 'Charles Lloyd', DNB, ed. Leslie Stephen and Sidney Lee, Vol. XI, p. 1290. London: OUP, 1909.

Day, E. Hermitage (ed), 'Letters from Oxford and Littlemore: An Unpublished Correspondence on the Oxford Movement.' *The Treasury*, 18 (October 1911), pp. 22–6, 119–24.

(Foulkes, Edmund S.) (pub. anonymously), *A History of the Church of St. Mary the Virgin, Oxford*. London: Longmans Green, 1892.

Guiney, Louise Imogen, *Hurrell Froude: Memoranda and Comments*. London: Methuen, 1904.

Härdelin, Alf, *The Tractarian Understanding of the Eucharist*. Uppsala: Acta Universitatis Upsalensis, 1965.

Jones, Owain W., *Isaac Williams and his Circle*. London: SPCK, 1971.

Lentini, Anselmo (ed), *Te Decet Hymnus: L'Innario della 'Liturgia Horarum'*. Vatican: Typis Polyglottis Vaticanis, 1984.

Liddon, H. P., *Life of Edward Bouverie Pusey*, 4 vols. London: Longmans Green, 1893–7.

Lockhart, William, 'Cardinal Newman: Or 'Tis Fifty Years Since'. *Dublin Review* (October 1890).

Middleton, R. D., *Magdalen Studies*. London: SPCK, 1936.

—— *Newman and Bloxam*, London: OUP, 1947

—— *Newman at Oxford: His Religious Development*. London: OUP, 1950.

Moseley, H. H. 'Newman and the Roman Breviary', *Worship* 34:2 (January 1960), pp. 75–8.

Mozley, Anne (ed), *Letters and Correspondence of J. H. Newman during his life in the English Church*, 2 vols. London: Longmans Green, 1890.

Murray, Placid, *Newman the Oratorian. His unpublished Oratory Papers, edited with an Introductory Study on the continuity between his Anglican and his Catholic ministry.* Dublin: Gill and Macmillan, 1969.

Newman, John Henry, *Apologia pro Vita Sua.* London: Longmans Green, 1873.

—— *Correspondence of John Henry Newman with John Keble and others 1839–1845*, ed. at the Birmingham Oratory. London: Longman, 1917.

—— *Hymni Ecclesiae e Breviario Parisiensi.* Oxford: J. H. Parker, 1838.

—— *Hymni Ecclesiae e Breviariis Romano, Sarisburiensi, Eboracensi et aliunde.* Oxford: J. H. Parker, 1839.

—— *John Henry Newman: Autobiographical Writings*, ed. Henry Tristram. London: Sheed and Ward, 1955.

—— *Lectures on Justification.* London: Rivington, 1838.

—— *Lectures on the Prophetical Office of the Church, viewed relatively to Romanism and popular Protestantism.* London: Rivington, 1837.

—— *Parochial Sermons*, 5 vols. London: Rivington, 1836.

—— *The Letters and Diaries of John Henry Newman*, ed. Charles Stephen Dessain and others. (See p. 153.)

—— *Verses on Various Occasions.* London: Longmans Green, 1867.

Newman, J. H. *and* Keble, J. (eds), *The Remains of the late Reverend Richard Hurrell Froude, M. A., Fellow of Oriel College, Oxford*, 2 parts (4 vols), London: Rivington, 1838–9.

Oakeley, Frederick, 'Historical Notes of the Tractarian Movement', *Dublin Review* (July 1863).

—— *Personal Reminiscences of the Oxford Movement.* Printed for the Islington Catholic Popular Club by Henry Teulon, 1855.

—— in *Reminiscences of Oxford by Oxford Men 1559–1850*, ed. Lilian M. Quiller-Couch [Oxford Historical Society XXII, 1892]. Oxford: Clarendon Press, 1892, pp. 324–8

Ollard, S. L. *A Short History of the Oxford Movement.* London: A. R. Mowbray, 2nd ed. rev. 1933.

Oxford, Members of the University of, *Tracts for the Times.* London: Rivington, 1833–41.

Palmer, William (Worcester College), *Origines Liturgicae.* London: Rivington, 1st ed. 1832, 4th ed. rev. 1845.

Pattison, Mark, *Memoirs*. London: Macmillan, 1888.

Prevost, George (ed), *Autobiography of Isaac Williams*. London: Longman, 3rd ed. 1893.

Salesian Fathers, *Newman and Littlemore: A Centenary Anthology and Appeal.* Oxford: The Salesian Fathers, Littlemore, 1945.

Sheridan, Thomas L., *Newman on Justification*. New York: Alba House, 1967.

Stanton, Richard, 'Some Reminiscences of the Early Days of Cardinal Newman's Life.' *Dublin Review* (October 1890).

Wheeler, Gordon (ed), *Homage to Newman 1845–1945*. Westminster Cathedral Chronicle, 1945.

(Williams, Isaac) *Hymns translated from the Parisian Breviary*. By the author of 'The Cathedral'. London: Rivington, 1839.

Williams, K. Mary, *The Doctrine of the Church in the writings of Isaac Williams 1802–1865*. University of London thesis. Published privately, 1983.

Index